So many doubts; so many worries. Sensory Processing Disorder is a family affair, not "just" a challenge that affects children.

Nowhere is this message more clear and poignant than in Michele Gianetti's new book, *I Believe In You*. Elizabeth is the child-protagonist, a resilient champion who eventually finds priceless and effective care, but no one is more devoted or steadfast than her mother, who advocates relentlessly for her baby...then for her big girl.

Michele's description of the journey of a parent and child with Sensory Processing Disorder is a classic tale. The constant second-guessing oneself...*What if I had only done X instead of Y or what if I hadn't done Z...would that have made a difference?* The moments of guilt, worry, anticipation, eagerness, despair...

What I love about this book is the poetry in prose and its unmitigated triumph over unending challenge. *Yes, parents, you can make a difference!* Ultimately this is a book of hope, a book describing the village needed to support children with Sensory Processing Disorder and their families, a book that sings of courage, anguish, joy, desolation, exhilaration, unforeseen disappointments, and expectations surpassed.

Michele asks, "Whose fault is it that this problem exists? Where does it come from? Was there something we could have done differently to avoid this pain?" Research suggests that except in extreme cases of pre-natal or post-natal neglect or abuse, Sensory Processing Disorder is not caused by the actions of loving, excited, and carebe before their child is born or after birth. The most common cause may be heritability, or more likely as with most behavioral and developmental disorders, caused by a gene and environment interaction. And, for as yet unknown reasons, certain children may be more susceptible than others to these genetic or environmental effects.

Speaking most to mothers and fathers of children with Sensory Processing Disorder, this is a book of reality, of hope, and of celebration for the small victories in the every day lives of families and their children with this disorder.

This book is a must-read for parents and therapists of children with Sensory Processing Disorder everywhere!
—Lucy Jane Miller, PhD, OTR Director,
STAR Center (Sensory Therapies and Research)
and Executive Director, Sensory Processing Disorder Foundation

i believe in
you

i believe in

a mother & daughter's
special journey

you

Michele Gianetti, R.N.

TATE PUBLISHING
AND ENTERPRISES, LLC

Published by Tate Publishing & Enterprises, LLC
127 E. Trade Center Terrace | Mustang, Oklahoma 73064 USA
1.888.361.9473 | www.tatepublishing.com

Tate Publishing is committed to excellence in the publishing industry. The company reflects the philosophy established by the founders, based on Psalm 68:11,
"The Lord gave the word and great was the company of those who published it."

Book design copyright © 2011 by Tate Publishing, LLC. All rights reserved.
Cover design by Kellie Vincent
Interior design by Lindsay B. Behrens

Published in the United States of America

ISBN: 978-1-61346-851-7
1. Biography & Autobiography / Medical
2. Biography & Autobiography / General
11.10.28

Dedication

This book is an act of love for my precious daughter, Elizabeth, to let the world know who she is, what she can do, and that she is loved so very much. I am so thankful to my mom and dad for their love and support, for without it I would have faltered so many times on this journey. Thank you for always being the safe haven I have known since forever. I love you both so very, very much. Thank you to my brothers, Marc and C.J., and C.J.'s wife, Lyn, for your love and laughter and for being right there for me to reach out to, to gain both strength and perspective through it all. You are the very parts of my heart. Thank you to Emily, for being the daughter a mother dreams about. Thank you for your love and kindness and friendship. I treasure you and adore you and love you so much. Thank you for being all you are for Elizabeth. Your gifts to her are simply priceless. Thank you to our little Michael, who unwittingly became the impetus for Elizabeth to soar as a big sister, and thank you for loving one of your *best friends* so much. And finally, thank you to my best friend and one and only love, John. Thank you for loving me through it all. Thank you for always being right there for me. I love you so very much. I love your ways, your smile, and your strength. Thank you for being just who I need each day. I pray for God's blessing for these people whom I love so much.

Acknowledgments

My first one is to my cousin and friend, Mary Carmen Kelly, who has been a constant source of help and support through this whole exciting process. She has spent countless hours helping me. I could not have done this without you. Thank you so much.

I would like to mention those wonderful people and organizations who have helped us in the order that they entered our journey. Thank you to Kathy, who was the first therapist to say, "I can help her." Thank you, Kathy, you are so special to us, and we love you.

To Maureen, who was our first O.T. and gave us such direction and hope. To Mary, for being one of the most important and wonderful friends and therapists we were blessed to have found. Thank you for your patience and love. Thank you, Dawn, for being a wonderful therapist and friend. Thank you to our Rosemarie. You are the best teacher and friend, we are blessed to have found you, and we love you. Thank you to Jill for your expertise in

CST. You have a great relationship with Elizabeth, and you have helped us all so much. Thank you to Terry, our trainer, who helped our Elizabeth succeed in the otherwise off-putting area we call physical education.

The following are the websites for the organizations we have used:

www.spdfoundation.net and
www.pdppro.com for Sensory Processing Disorder
www.dyspraxiausa.org for dyspraxia
www.upledger.com for cranial-sacral therapy
www.advancedbrain.com for the listening program
www.talktools.com

Table of Contents

Foreword

Many of us are fortunate to grow up in families that pass down unique expertise from one generation to the next. I am one of the fortunate ones, as a third generation member of the Doman family, which has contributed to the growing body of information on child brain development since the 1940s, with a mission centered on helping people achieve their unique and extraordinary potential.

My early training was as an infant, a recipient of brain training methods developed by my grandfather, great-uncle, father, and their colleagues, each brilliant visionaries and advocates for children. Today my wife and I apply the same philosophy to our infant son Brendan's development. This philosophy centers on the understanding that the human brain is an unfinished sculpture which takes shape based on our genes, environment, and experiences. As parents we can influence environment and experience, and we are the experts. "Parents are the world's greatest experts on their children" is to me one of my father's most memorable quotes.

Through Advanced Brain Technologies (ABT), the company I founded in 1998, it has been my great fortune to know many special needs children, their parents, and the professionals helping to guide them. Many of these exceptional children have surpassed others' expectations of who they were, who they would become, and what they could achieve. Feats such as walking, talking, seeing, listening, reading, and playing, that are easy for most, were considered impossible for these special kids I've known through the years. These kids achieved the extraordinary because their parents saw the unique potential within their children and did everything within their power to help them become even more extraordinary.

I Believe in You is a hopeful, funny, and at times painfully candid chronicle of a family with a special child. From the outside, the Gianetti family looks like they are living the American dream. The father is a successful physician, the mother a stay-at-home mom with a bachelor's degree in nursing, and together they have three beautiful children. However, their second child, Elizabeth, demonstrated from her earliest moments that looks can be deceiving, and that life with an exceptional child is at times filled with confusion, frustration, and sorrow. Confusion as her parents try to understand what is wrong, frustration with how to fix the problems, and sorrow because they want their child to have a happy, productive, and fulfilling life, and they were not sure that she ever would.

Dyspraxia and Sensory Integration Dysfunction are two of the terms used to describe Elizabeth's challenges. Dyspraxia is a disorder of the brain and nervous system in which a person is unable to perform tasks or movements when asked to do so. The person understands the request or command and is willing to perform the task, the muscles needed to perform the task work properly, and the task may have been learned already, but the person cannot accomplish it. Something that is easy for you or me to do, such as using a fork and knife or speaking clearly, can be seemingly impossible for someone with dyspraxia.

Sensory Integration Dysfunction (SID), more recently called Sensory Processing Disorder (SPD), is a brain disorder characterized by difficulty organizing sensory information as it comes in through the senses. According to researchers at the Sensory Processing Disorder Foundation, sensory information may be sensed and perceived by people with SPD in a way that is different from most people. The difference is that information is often registered, interpreted, and then processed differently by the brain of someone with SPD than it is by normal individuals. The result can be unusual ways of responding or behaving as well as finding tasks harder to do. Findings in SPD typically present as difficulties in planning and organizing, problems with the activities of everyday life (self-care, work, leisure activities, and play), and, for those with severe sensitivity to sensory input, such input may result in agitation, distress, fear, confusion, or even extreme avoidance of activities.

These descriptions will be all too familiar to many of the parents reading this book. So, too, will Michele Gianetti's account of her family's journey, attempting to navigate a maze of physicians, therapists, schools, interventions, and diets. You might think that this would be easy for parents who are medical professionals, but Michele would likely say that is not the case. Elizabeth's needs led her, her parents, and her siblings on an odyssey with many detours and no roadmap. *I Believe in You* charts their course through a labyrinth of physicians, occupational therapy, speech and language pathology, Individualized Education Programs, sensory diets, craniosacral therapy, biomedical treatments, and more.

Elizabeth's mom, Michele, contacted me to see if I would review what she has written about The Listening Program® (TLP), and then later she gave me the honor of reading the manuscript and writing this foreword, something which I did not hesitate to say yes to. The Listening Program® is a music listening therapy I co-developed with ABT. Michele was fortunate to have a most innovative speech and language pathologist named Mary introduce her to The Listening Program® and guide her as Elizabeth's provider. TLP helped Elizabeth process sensory information better, and it continues to be an important part of her life today.

If you are a parent, especially the parent of an exceptional child, please read this book. *I Believe in You* will be an inspiration. It will inspire you to trust your instincts, to seek second opinions, and to advocate for and always believe in your child's extraordinary potential.

—Alex Doman, Founder and CEO Advanced Brain Technologies
Author, *Healing at the Speed of Sound*

Introduction

They say autism is in epidemic proportions these days. But what about the kids who sort of fall into the spectrum? The ones who meet some but not all of the criteria? The ones who have other conditions? Conditions just like autism. As a parent of one of those children, I know how very frustrating and exhausting it is trying to get the world around you to understand just what your child has and how they "work." I want to share the story of our life with such a child in a way that is easy to read, one that is both humorous and serious. I want to tell about the therapies we tried, the different therapists we have seen, the medications and supplements. I want to share all we did to help our daughter. Maybe this story, our story, will touch someone else with a child like ours. Someone who needs to know another family is out there living a problem they thought no one else had. Maybe someone will read about a certain therapy, and maybe they will try it for their own child.

In the beginning, we did not have a list of things to try; we had to find them on our own. I want to share the experience because it was so lonely and scary being the only mom I knew with a child like Elizabeth. A child who acted in ways she and only she did. Whenever we were with other kids, I would scan, look, and evaluate their behaviors, trying so hard to see if any child acted in any way like Elizabeth. It was like I desperately needed to know that she was not the only one. But when I looked around, I just kept seeing a world of typically developing children and their happy mothers.

She is now thirteen years old, a happy and growing child. She has also worked so hard for every new task she has ever accomplished and every word she has ever said. She has taken our family on a journey that no one could have guessed we would be on. A journey that, when we look behind us, seems so full of twists and turns and, when we look ahead, is uncharted.

This story is also about the survival of our family. Each and every member has been challenged by this child and her journey. Our strength comes from faith and prayers and in the form of family, therapists, teachers, and friends who have joined us on this journey. We have had so many special people join us on this walk and share their gifts to help our daughter. Through all this, we have found that our strength runs deeper than we ever could have imagined.

The First Signs of a Problem

Elizabeth has two major conditions that affect her each and every day. She works so hard at so many things that I have always said she is the hardest working child I have ever met. Elizabeth is a child with both sensory processing disorder and dyspraxia. At this point I feel it is important to note that professionals have differing opinions on whether sensory processing disorder and dyspraxia are linked as one, or can be separated into two distinct categories. Although they are closely related, in my book I have chosen to separate them, as that is how we could best address all of her needs.

Either of these conditions could make learning and achieving developmental milestones a challenge, but both together make it incredibly harder. Dyspraxia is a condition involving motor planning, such as using scissors. For a typically developing child, you show them, they watch you, try it a few times, and then they learn the skill. For Elizabeth, someone shows it to her and then each and every step from the placement of the fingers to how to squeeze the scissors are shown to her again and again. She will learn the task, but only after many, many attempts. Each and every skill has to be broken down for her and repeated countless times to aid her success. And we are still working on new skills. It is a huge job and challenge.

Elizabeth's dyspraxia is global, meaning it affects all muscles, including those that help her talk. (Her first real word was at the age of five.) The second condition is SPD, and it involves the way her body accepts sensory input, from heat to cold to touch to even wearing shoes (we could not get shoes on her little feet for the longest time when she was a baby). Her neurological system inputs the sensory information, but it can't process what she feels the way "we" do. It all feels "wrong" or "offensive" to her. Occupational therapy to integrate or introduce sensory information to her body has been a part of her life since she was two-and-a-half years old. All sensory information is introduced a little at a time, over time, to allow her to get used to it and accept the sensation instead of rejecting it and sometimes actually running away from it.

I think now is the time to start at the very beginning of this story: me, pregnant with Elizabeth. She was born June 29, 1997.

I can still remember when the test stick turned positive for my second pregnancy. I was never good at surprising my husband with a teddy bear, saying, "Aww! You are going to be a dad again!" Nope. For me it's, "Oh my God! Look! Here is the stick!"

So after the heart-warming moment, I tossed my cream stick donut and coffee in the trash and vowed to eat healthfully for this baby, and I think I did. I took the prenatal vitamins, drank lots of water, and toned down the exercise just like before. I will admit that gaining weight is a difficult thing for me to accept. And, yes, I complained a lot and made a little too big of a deal about it, but in the end I was okay with it because it was good for this baby. All went well until the twelfth week, and I got the flu. And that is the first of many things that started me wondering about causes of Elizabeth's conditions. I will always wonder if this virus that really felled me, and the 101.4 temperature that it created in me, caused any problems for this baby. The doctor says no, that we were in the second trimester, etc. But how can you really know? I will always wonder and think about it. I suppose in heaven I will be able to receive my answers. It is hard to have this feeling of regret over something I had no control over.

After that episode, things went pretty well. The typical nausea and tiredness, etc. We were happy that all looked well on the sonogram at twenty weeks. Time passed, and then we got the very unhappy news that my doctor was getting knee surgery done and would be leaving the office to the care of someone else at exactly my time to deliver.

We were upset and thought about switching to a new group, but we did not do it. Our doctor had delivered Emily, and we felt she would never steer us wrong.

The replacement doctor had no real vested interest in me, my husband, or the baby; she was helping out a colleague. She saw me in her office one time before I went into labor. My labors are those of horror movies. They last days and days and are so slow to progress that we have literally seen the nurses switch shifts at least two times per each labor. I felt the contractions starting Wednesday night. They were about ten to fifteen minutes apart, but they were regular. I called the new doctor, and she said instead of coming in to the hospital, just keep walking and watching the contractions, and when they got closer together to call her back. So labor began Wednesday night, and I did not go to the hospital until Saturday night. Elizabeth was born Sunday at 12:55 p.m. (Yes, that is correct.)

Was all that time in early labor and walking around really okay? Should I have asked to be checked? Or should I have been told to come in? Only God knows. I just cannot believe the perfect storm of events. It really does play on one's thoughts. If we could change one thing—go back and vary the doctor or not get the flu or go to the hospital earlier—would it have mattered? I think moms of special needs children do wonder how it happened. Was it something they did or did not do? I know in my case, I question what made it occur, and maybe I just wish I had done better for her. Maybe I failed her in some way with the decisions I made, and I would love the chance to go back and correct those things.

Okay, back to the hospital and my labor. My epidural was started and did not numb correctly, so more medicine was given, once then twice. I had numbness in one-half my body and felt all in the other half. Was this extra medicine going to our baby? And was it hurting her? After the doctor broke my water, she left to make rounds at another institution. She had to be called back to deliver Elizabeth. She made it just in time. I know that she did not do anything overtly wrong, but her handling of the situation was less than caring. And when Elizabeth was placed on my tummy, she had not been suctioned and she was bluish. I remember asking them, "Don't you think you should suction her?" And then they did, and *then* she cried. Precious moments lost. And yet again, I wonder about its effects on Elizabeth. But, oh my God, was she cute! Chubby and round and squeezy. I was happy, the baby appeared normal and healthy, and all was good until just the second day of her life.

Before I can talk about the very first frightening sign of a problem, I so need to say that denial is a great big force to fight. I lived in it for a long, long time. And what is truly ironic is that I am a nurse, my husband, John, is a doctor, and yet we denied so much. We were taught about illnesses and conditions. Yet we did not want to see, or maybe more accurately, could not allow ourselves to see what was really going on. We had no reason to think that there would or could be a problem. Our first born, Emily, was a dream. Happy, laughing, hugging, growing faster than the books tell you. We would soon see it would not be that way with Elizabeth.

I remember getting up Monday, one day after Elizabeth's birth, showering and getting ready to call the nursery. They would then "deliver" the baby to my room. I felt great that day until I saw the face of the nurse. She said "Whew! You take her for a while, she's a real hand-ful!" And she walked away. My heart clutched, and my stomach instantly became sick. I later came to understand that she screamed all night and all morning in the nursery. I don't know what they tried to do to calm her, or if it even worked at all. Now understand, these are veteran nurses who work in the newborn nursery, with crying babies all day and night; *our* baby sent them over the edge. I held her that day and, yes, she cried a lot, and it was a very shrill, high-pitched cry. A very scary cry. Yes, she was very hard to console. Elizabeth did not like to be put down, but I reasoned that she was a newborn who just liked to be held. Now, with a clear head, I remember that her older sister, Emily, was perfectly fine being put down or put in a little chair.

Elizabeth and I were discharged the next day, and we went home to her big sister and my mom and dad. We all had dinner together, and it was a fun homecoming. Elizabeth was quite quiet that night, and I thought, "Whew, that nurse was wrong, thank God!"

The next day, my mom stayed most of the day. Then she left, and I swear, that was the last peaceful morning I had in a long, long time. After my mom went home, I tried to put Elizabeth in a little bouncy chair so I could play with Emily, and she cried; I tried to put her on a soft blanket. She cried. I decided that I would carry her to keep her happy, but she still cried. It was getting to be clear to me that she was a crier, but why so much? And why all the time?

I did not have extra time to think all this through, because life goes on with a two-and-a-half year old. Emily needed me, and I wanted her home to be peaceful. Emily was great with the baby from the start. She was, however, getting a little tired of the crying, and then the resulting carrying. I never had my hands free those first few days. I can so very clearly see the signs of her sensory issues now as I look back. All things overwhelmed her tiny neurological system. She could not be out of my arms to feel anything. The sensations were too much for her, and she would cry. After the first couple weeks, I fell into a routine of carrying her everywhere, and it seemed to work. Emily was happy; Elizabeth was, for the most part, content. But it really wasn't the way it was supposed to be. I would just say to myself, "Tomorrow I will put her down, and it will be better." That tomorrow never came.

Elizabeth was born in the summer, so I thought initially that the warm weather would make it easier with a newborn, such as walks and swing time outside, but it wasn't so. I will always remember our first walk; Elizabeth was two or three weeks old, and we had a brand new double stroller. I was so happy to use it. Emily loved her walks and was happy to sit in the front and see the world, and I thought Elizabeth would love the motion of the stroller while she was reclined and cozy in the back. We have a lovely street, a bit under a mile in length, and it was a beautiful morning. I fed the girls, and we set out.

We only got as far as four houses away when Elizabeth started to cry, and I mean cry. I stopped and put her pacifier in and started again. Now she was screaming so loudly and would not stop, so I had to take her out, hold her, and push a double stroller with a toddler in it back home. One neighbor joked, "Did you just pinch her or what?"

Ha-ha, you be me for a bit, and then we can talk is what I was thinking, but instead I smiled. I was told by a therapist later that Elizabeth was really unable to take in all the sensory information around her that day. Such as the breezes, the sun, the vibrations of the road. So she had no way to enjoy it all, and the result is that she needed to be held and in that way, those sensations were lessened and in some way she was settled. She really did not want to be part of this world unless it involved my arms carrying her all day, every day.

As weeks moved into months, Elizabeth continued to be a puzzle to my husband, John, and me. We just could not believe that a little one could be so upset all the time. Elizabeth was a beautiful baby with huge, blue eyes and curly, brown hair. She was chubby and all people wanted to do was hug her, but she did not really like to be hugged or touched too much. She looked like nothing should be wrong with her. Elizabeth's doctor dismissed our concerns and just called her a "fussy baby." But it was way more than that. All the ways we had cared for Emily as a baby only made Elizabeth cry.

When Emily was getting ready to take a nap or go to bed, we had the room softly lit, and she had a bottle. We rocked her a bit, and then she was placed in her crib. Not so for Elizabeth. What stands out the most with Elizabeth was that in order for her to sleep, she needed to be held close but rocked, almost in a vibrating way. She would not settle down in any other fashion. It seemed so odd to me, but we did it.

We learned to do things "Elizabeth's way" very quickly. When a child has sensory processing disorder, their bodies crave the kind of sensory information that calms them, and in this case the shaking and vibrating feeling was "it" for her. Odd how the "normal" sensations made her pull away from the world, but a sensation that other babies would dislike was the ultimate for her system.

I can remember a specific day when my mom and grandma had come over to visit, and just how difficult Elizabeth was that day. Now my mom and grandma both have years of kid experience and beautiful, kind ways. But it was at a fussy time for Elizabeth, and she was fussier than usual. Maybe because this was near to her naptime, but she just would not settle. I tried to lie with her on the couch and kind of crook her in my arms and vibrate her. It did not work. I finally gave up and handed her to my mom, who I swear has one of the most calming, beautiful touches in the world. As a child I can remember just feeling so loved and often better just by my mom touching me. Even she could not get Elizabeth to stop fussing. There was such a look of concern in my mom's face as we all were basically out of ideas as to what this fed, changed, rocked, and loved child could possibly need. Sadly, it was by fussing and crying to exhaustion that she finally fell asleep.

Some days she fell asleep better than others, but I think it was because she was happy to use naptime as an escape from the world of sounds, smells, and sensations that she could not cope with.

When I realized that Elizabeth liked the vibrating sensation, I found out that the bouncy chairs came with that option. Just flip a switch, and instant shaking. That chair and my sanity went hand in hand. She *loved* it, and she would sit in it forever if I let her. At first I did, and may I say I kept us in enough D cell batteries to work that chair through Armageddon. But then I felt so bad because I started to realize that she hated being out of it more after she was in it for a long time. So, yes, on one hand we had peace but on the other hand, we had a false peace and one that weighed heavily on my mind. She could not live in that bouncy chair and be part of our lives or part of this world. It made me feel bad for her. I wanted her happy in our world.

I will tell you this: when your heart tells you something, when your being tells you something, when you feel something so deeply…listen to it…those feelings are there for a reason. I feel they are God's intercessions to my mind and, when they were followed I felt peaceful, like I was doing the right thing and was on the right track. So I was feeling bad about Elizabeth in the chair and realized for the *first* time ever that we were going to have to find ways to get her to cope in this world. Now keep in mind, at this time we had no idea what she had, or *if* she had anything or even how to help her.

For that matter, it literally was just this feeling I had so deep in my soul that I knew weaning her away from that chair was what we had to do for her. So the chair went off except for small amounts of time. I could see that small doses of it helped her feel calm in our world for a while. And then we began navigating just what to do to help her cope each day—some time in her chair, and then into the world, also known as our den. It was not easy to do this, but that feeling inside me never left, and it helped me through each day and each little victory, like when she cried less, or looked less afraid, just reinforced it.

I know we continued on as best we could each day. I held her, took care of Emily, and played down the fear that we were really in some situation that was terrifying. As Elizabeth aged a bit and was about three to four months, about the time kids start to lift their heads to roll over or just play during "tummy time," we got another eye-opening of the dyspraxia portion of Elizabeth's problems. She could not keep her head up long at all. I remembered that with time, Emily got better and better at it, which of course is the goal, but not with Elizabeth. It was like her little head weighed so much, and her arms did not want to support her. We stayed near her at this tummy time because her little face would literally end up in the blanket if we did not. Now we were concerned. Where was her muscle control?

Then we realized she was not really grabbing at things much. She would kind of bat at them. It almost looked like a kitten hitting a ball of yarn. So we knew she could see things and could recognize there was something fun there, but that was it. She also could not sit up in a high-chair well at all, even with blanket rolls on either side of her. It became increasingly clear that she needed help with her muscle control and in developing those muscles; I never thought a baby would not just do these things on their own. We had to help her each day to grow stronger and master these little milestones that for Emily came as naturally as her next smile.

We would sit by her and hold her arms in the right position during tummy time so that her weight was well distributed, and each day we would do more until she got it. We did the same with the highchair, giving her a little time un-propped, and then a little more until she gained strength and she got it. We could see different needs and help her. The common thread here is that with help and practice she did meet the goals, but it was hard and long. And here is the big piece: we were always fighting her sensory issues too. So something new, with its feelings and sensations, etc., was scary to her anyway. Combine that with a new task, using new muscles.

It was hard work for her each day. We were fighting many factors. I think truly the only reason we had success was a combination of this knowledge that repetition and practice worked and a deep drive to help her meet these milestones. We had to make those things happen, and by doing so, we sort of hit on how Elizabeth would be making "all" her hard fought gains in life.

What Doesn't She Cry About?
Where Are the Milestones?

As I begin to write about this next topic, I can still feel my helplessness. As Elizabeth got older, about five months old or so, and the world began to open up for her, there was a definite increase in her anxiety level. As I said, her system does not properly process information, and it was coming in at her in great amounts. She liked to watch the shapes on the TV, but would cry if I left her alone with the TV on. She hated her baths. She screamed when she was touched by the water. She hated some articles of clothing. She cried in the seats at the grocery store. She cried in restaurants, the library, and even at my parents' house.

She was, in essence, scared of the whole world. And the *only* thing that kept her somewhat quiet was my arms. I had to carry her all day. Even in our home, I learned to do everything, even laundry, one-handed (which was no easy feat with a top loading machine). I kept thinking that one time she is just going to slide right in with the dirty laundry if I wasn't careful. I even learned to color with Emily while still holding Elizabeth. I kept my resolve of wanting to help Elizabeth cope in our world, but it seemed to become harder as her anxiety increased. If I even left her line of vision, she screamed and would not stop until she saw me and I held her. It was bad.

It was breakfast time, and Emily was sitting at the kitchen table, Elizabeth was in her highchair, propped up as usual, and I was nervous, as usual. I found myself getting this nervous feeling a lot because I was never sure how the day would go, or how long Elizabeth would sit, or when she would start screaming. So there we were. Emily was munching breakfast when she turned to me and said, "Mommy, I need more milk for my cereal." And I could just feel my stomach clutch and I thought, *I cannot get up to get it, I cannot get up and risk setting off a crying fit from Elizabeth.* A simple walk to the refrigerator was too much for me to handle. I would be just out of her sight long enough to send her system into panic mode. I was her security, and that was it. So I sadly told Emily that she probably didn't need any more milk in her cereal. And I stayed right where I was for reasons that only I knew. It was clear at that moment that I was changing as a person each day. I did not even realize fully until then that I had, for the past five months, slowly been doing things Elizabeth's way. I was sad that morning. For Emily, with no milk, for myself, and for Elizabeth.

I would come to see that there would be many more mornings just like that one. Then, I got an idea. I would put *everything* I thought Emily would want, or potentially need, on the table before we would sit down for breakfast. I told her it was like a buffet. She could pick up her own things. She loved it and thought it was fun. To me it looked like the complimentary breakfast at the Hampton Inns and Suites®. But it worked. I was relieved and thought that I had been able to create some calm in the mornings. I seemed to be using the word *calm* a great deal. But I guess to me, calm is the goal of each day, and it signifies we are all organized within ourselves and peaceful inside. This then allows the calm to be shown in our home. To this day, I still strive for and love calm.

At this time of her life, Elizabeth was very anxious and very on guard all the time. It was like she was waiting for the next assault on her system. She made sure she kept a close eye on me and my whereabouts. The assaults for Elizabeth could come in all forms, even those of new foods. She was a good eater if the food was soft and not very textured. She also showed a symptom of gastric problems by spitting up at least one or more ounces of her bottle feedings. This was why I was excited to start her on rice cereal and then food. I was thinking that the textures and thickness would help her keep food down and help her feel full and, of course, maybe calm. She would get upset if a new food were offered, and she quickly, without words, made it clear which things were her favorite and which ones were not.

I can remember that we used distractions a great deal to feed her. It was best if I could time the food to be ready when an intro to a show came on. They would sing, and I would feed her, and she would eat. The song would end, and she would be a lot more difficult to feed. She would gag a great deal or have trouble manipulating the food in her mouth. This was due to her oral dyspraxia, or poor motor planning, of her muscles in her mouth. *We* chew and swallow, but *she* had trouble with even the slightest of textured foods. I actually rearranged the kitchen a bit to angle her toward the TV. Welcome to meal time at our house. I made sure Emily was next to her and, of course, Emily thought it was great having television with dinner. Yeah, team! Just for the record, I grew to hate whatever was on TV at 4:00 p.m.

Oddly, in my journal I wrote that she loves hard bread. I wrote this over and over. Odd though, for a baby who gagged on most things to love the hard bread so much. Now I understand why. She loved the sensory input it gave her system to bite it and bite it. It felt good to her system and kind of calmed her. To this day, when she is frustrated or nervous she will clench her jaws tight and, at times, bite her hand. She gets in trouble for that one, though. Here was yet another sign of her SPD. Ahh! So clear in retrospect and, of course, years of therapy later. Mealtime was the only time that distraction worked for

Elizabeth. Otherwise, she was extremely focused on the anxiety-provoking "new" thing. And she would not, could not, be distracted.

So for a quick review, we are now into the tenth and eleventh months of her life. She is just now starting to sit up well on her own. In my journal, I wrote that she was starting to scoot a bit, like a worm. I do remember that she did not use her arms much and only raised her little hind-end up and down. Where were those other muscles? As we continued to navigate the first year, I noted that she was babbling but not saying anything remotely like "da-da" at all. If I could have seen into the future at this point, I would have probably dropped to my knees to see just how bad it was going to get, and how much work we were going to have to do, and just how big a toll it was going to take on me and my mental state. Just as an uplifting sidebar here: as I write this sentence, I hear my sweet Elizabeth singing the *Spongebob Squarepants*® theme.

My stomach gets ill as I write our past, but when I look up and see our present, I know *everything* we did was worth it. That every step was important. Each thing was like a piece of the big puzzle. The puzzle is coming together well but still has missing pieces that I am sure we will have to find as she gets older. All things happen for a reason, and in a time that they are meant to happen. If you are trying something and it isn't working, don't be afraid to change it. And talk to your therapist, think it through, and follow your heart. But do not beat yourself up for the time spent on a previous therapy. It may have done its job at a time when it was needed. And now it is not needed anymore, so a new one must be tried or a new avenue explored.

We have found many therapists, therapies, and supplements. And now that we look back, I sometimes say, "Why didn't we try that earlier?" or "Hey, why did we wait until she was five to do this?" I believe you go with your heartfelt choice, believing it is right for your child for this moment. I try not to let myself do the hindsight review and feel bad. I always tell myself that we did what was best for Elizabeth at that time in her life.

I speak a great deal about following your feelings and being strong about them because early on I was not as strong as I am now. A huge point to illustrate this is that I allowed, or rather, gladly accepted, the pediatrician's statements that she was just on the late end of the developmental scale. I wish I could go back as I am now and say, "Tell me when I should start testing," or "Why does she do this or act this particular way?"

The doctor did the normal well-baby checkup, and Elizabeth cried like most kids do. But even if I said, "She is like this all the time," they did not take my concerns to heart. And when I said she is not doing this or that, they would tell me she is just on the late side of developing. We did have Elizabeth immunized and, very clearly, she was receiving mercury or thimerosol in her vaccines, just by the fact that she received them in 1997–1998. I am not saying they created the problem in my child, I am saying they were one more thing in her body that she could not deal with. It was one more thing that we maybe could have controlled so she could have developed without having to fight its effects. And let's be clear on this, these problems she has were certainly there way, way before she received any vaccines. Having said this, I wish we could have at least taken this variable out of the mix for her, though I remember leaving the offices after each well-baby visit and for a very brief—very brief—moment, feeling relieved from the doctor's words. *My* relief lasted only until she started screaming in the car as I closed her door to go to the driver's side, and thus was once again out of her line of vision. Then my whole stomach would clench, and I would realize once again that John and I were really on our own in this game.

We still had no idea or guidance to help her. Time was passing, and it was like all the other babies born on her date were on the second lap of the track, and she was still just out of the blocks. Catching up seemed so impossible as she resisted all new things. We had to keep trying to get her to accomplish even the littlest things, like holding a crayon. And if we could, we rejoiced. I hate to say it, but at a certain level we were simply in survival mode. Keep Elizabeth happy. Pray for her, pray for Emily to be peaceful and to have a happy home. Pray for God's strength for us each day. Every day!

When Will She Walk, Talk, or Try Something New?

As Elizabeth celebrated her first birthday, she did not really celebrate it. We had a very big party and all of our family came over but *she* did not enjoy the day, or rejoice. If anything, she looked extra nervous. She did not open one gift, did not even try to open any, did not like the paper, the boxes, or the bows. Most one-year-olds love to play and wrinkle paper and mouth things. She did nothing of the sort, and, sadly, we have this all on video to see just how she was on this day. We all made the day fun but in a weird way, as if we recognized her lack of participation and we all made up for it for her. Elizabeth does not possess natural curiosity. She does not desire to find out how something works, as it involves too much for her system to handle. Too much motor planning for her muscles and too much sensory information for her to voluntarily process. This last tidbit of knowledge comes after years and years of therapy.

We have, as I am writing this, a beautiful, typically-developing three-year-old who could make a day's worth of activity out of yesterday's newspaper and a dump truck. Michael is the very essence of natural curiosity, and as I watch him develop, I see all that Elizabeth did not do and did not achieve on her own. Sometimes I have to take a pause as I watch him because I see him do something on his own, and remember the day that an O.T. had to teach Elizabeth the same thing. Only for her, it was three years after he learned on his own. I wanted to use Emily as a marker to measure growth and development for Elizabeth, but I never could make myself do that because it was too painful to compare Elizabeth to Emily, as she was always ahead of the developmental chart. Emily was and always is such a source of peace and love. She loved her sister from the start, and they are close to this day.

At the age of one, a child should be walking or attempting to pull themselves up. They should be saying one or more words. They should be curious, and love to play and be read to. Elizabeth did not walk, she had no interest in it, and she did not play. She would hold a crayon and swipe it on paper, but that was it. We kept encouraging her to walk, trying to hold her up just like we trained her to do when she was trying to sit up. But it did not work.

It was so hard to do anything with her. If I took her to the store, she would scream in the cart. If I took her to the library, I would have to pretend to have fun while holding her, knowing we had only a few minutes until she would cry, and then I would be forced to leave. I prayed Emily never noticed my nerves, but, man, were they always firing. I was tense everywhere we went. I knew that once she started crying, she would not stop; I knew we needed to get in and out of a place as fast as possible. I would literally stand in line and sweat if it moved too slowly, and then I would shake if she started to cry, because once she started she could not be stopped.

And let's not forget I also had a three-year-old to keep an eye on, and I had to make sure that Emily had happy days. I vowed it could not be all about Elizabeth's need to be in my arms. We had to give Emily a happy life and get Elizabeth into the real world.

Elizabeth finally walked at eighteen months and, after two visits, with three X-rays from a pediatric orthopedist, Elizabeth would drag her left leg while she pushed a toy, and it was so sad to watch. We thought that was the reason for the delay in her walking. We were sent home that day with a "she'll walk when she wants to" diagnosis. In this case he was correct, and to this day we still do not know the reason for the left foot drag or why it went away. Time passed, and each day seemed to be the same as the one before; I would pretend for Emily that all was well, and then be dying inside to know that not only were things not well, they were very, very wrong. I would pray outside of Elizabeth's room each morning before I would enter and say, "Please, God, let today be the day she is better. Let today be the day she grows." But it never was that day. I thought once she walked that the rest would come, that she would just take off and we would be on our way.

We had two Christmases that seemed identical to each other, when Elizabeth was six months old, and again when she was one-and-a-half years old. She did not care what gift she got, she only cared that I was near her and never out of her sight. It was so hard watching everyone bringing her something, because she simply was not curious about the present, never grabbing it or exploring it. My family tried so hard to engage her, and all attempts fell flat. This was so clearly her sensory defensiveness coming out, and she could not get past it to try to explore something. She was smiling and happy only if she did not have to do or touch anything.

My mom always made a beautiful buffet dinner for most holidays. We would get our food in the kitchen and then sit in the dining room to eat. I so many times remember wanting to make a return trip to the kitchen table for food and having to sneak out while someone distracted Elizabeth because when she noticed I was gone, she would cry and try to get out of her highchair. That was so hard for my mom and dad to see, and I could just read the pain in their eyes when it occurred.

If Elizabeth did want to try a toy, her dyspraxia would prevent her from discovering the toy itself. She could not tell her hands to manipulate it this way or that, or to try to change a shoe on a doll. I see so clearly now how she must have felt when we were all saying to her, "Come on, try this" or "Let's play this." To her it was pressure, plain and simple, and she just could not escape all that held her back.

When someone has these two disorders, so much of their mind and energies are spent trying to cope in the basic day-to-day flow of the world that they really have no room to try to input more data and/or deal with a new food, toy, person, or just have fun. It would be easy to see how a child would want so much to escape the world, with all its fears and challenges, instead of pushing forward. It simply must be exhausting for them.

I read an article once that said in order to get an idea of a day in the life of a SPD child, wear your itchiest, high-neck sweater, turn your heat up high, have music that you hate blaring loudly, sit in a wooden chair that has one leg removed, and then try to talk to someone intelligently. I guess what I learned from that example is that these children not only can't process sensory information well, it would seem the information is magnified and almost screaming at them throughout their days. One thing that backs this up for me is that Elizabeth loved being in her dark room, in her crib. Quiet, dark, and alone. This brings me to the biggest turning point for me: the pool story.

Elizabeth was about two years old, and we were still in a place of wishful thinking and a degree of denial. That was decreasing, though, as reality was taking its place very sadly and quite efficiently. It was a hot, beautiful day, and we decided to put up the kiddie pool for the first time in the season. Emily was all thumbs-up and ready with her floaty ring. We set the pool up, and as I was doing this, I placed Elizabeth on the grass to sit, and she screamed. I placed her in the stroller to finish, and she screamed. Finally, John had the pool ready, and we put her in it—she screamed so loud, you would've thought the water was boiling hot and not just warm. By contrast, our Emily was happily floating around in it and loving the day.

There it was ... two children, only two and a half years apart, but separated by an abyss that was infinite. It was then and there that I knew in my heart of hearts that this child was ill and she needed help, or we would lose her. We would lose her as sure as I was standing there, hating that hot day. We would lose her to "her" world. Her world that was an easy escape from it all. For the record, the only thing that would stop her screams this time was putting her in a dark room, alone and cool, and even though it was not naptime yet, she was finally happy and quiet.

I was telling my dear friend Denise, who is also Elizabeth's godmother, about the pool story, and she in turn told me one sentence that changed our paths and our lives for Elizabeth. We are wonderful, close friends, but even then she tells me how scared she was to tell me.

All she said was, "Elizabeth has Sensory Integration Dysfunction" (now called Sensory Processing Disorder). "She needs help, or you will lose her."

That was it, that sentence was out there, and it was the beginning of our true path to finding help for Elizabeth. Without Denise's courage to say those words, we would have had no beginning to help this child.

I called Easter Seals soon after my talk with Denise, as she had worked there previously. I talked to a therapist about SPD. I can remember practically begging her to tell me over the phone, "Did Elizabeth have it or not?" Of course, she couldn't tell me, but then she mentioned the name of a therapist in our area who was one of the best OT's in the field then known as Sensory Integration Dysfunction. I called her workplace, and they told me she was on maternity leave, but they did say they would give her my number.

In three months, sure enough, Maureen actually called me back. Can you imagine how great that was? I mean, think about how many messages there must have been. But she called me. I was so happy to unburden myself to her and get her opinion. There just had to be a higher power at work here. God was guiding this for sure.

I need to again say to trust your instincts and yourself, and realize that all things happen when they are supposed to. Because after my initial call to Easter Seals, I remember going to John and talking through some other things about Elizabeth that were bothering me. I shared that sometimes she cried when I read to her, like a frustration, or she would not turn when something loud happened. That bothered me a great deal.

As a sidebar, she always acknowledged when her name was called or used. We decided that we need to take her to an ENT, or an ear, nose, and throat specialist, to see if there was a medical reason for these problems. We made an appointment with a specialist in town. The appointment was thorough, long, and stressful, because Elizabeth was so hard to work with. She cried a great deal and was hard to control through most of it, but the bottom line was that she had a huge amount of wax in her ears and he thought transient fluid was the problem.

He removed it and followed up that procedure with a tympanogram to measure the movement of the eardrum. Hers showed a nice mountain-like peak on the test strip, and in both ears too! I was happy and relieved. If someone has a flat line on the test strip, that indicates the eardrum is not moving well, and that may indicate that fluid is present in the ear. If she had fluid, it would have been treated at the doctor's discretion either with antibiotics, if the ear drum looked cloudy and she had pain and/or a temperature, or maybe with a decongestant, if the eardrum was bulging but not cloudy.

The doctor said he would be happy to check her as often as I wanted to record whether or not fluid was present. By doing this, we could see if she met the criteria to get tubes in her ears. I was happy to hear this because we had already documented a series of bilateral ear infections with our pediatrician. So we definitely needed to catch the fluid early and often to allow her to hear and to begin to talk.

Well, we were on our way. What a day! She cried so much, and the office felt so hot to me and so closed in that I was hugely relieved to be in the car on the way home. I put some music on to liven things up, and our little wonder screamed so loud that I realized the music was too loud for her ears. Now that the wax was removed, she could *hear!* I was so happy and felt that we had straightened out at least one variable for her.

I will say for a while she did not show any signs of fluid or discomfort. I took her in for a checkup one month after the initial appointment. At that point, she was okay. Keep in mind that she was still nonverbal at this point, and I kept thinking that without hearing words and inflections in voices, she would stand no chance of learning to talk. So each month I took her to the ENT, and sometimes she had fluid and sometimes she did not.

Over time, she did have many ear infections and, of course, so many rounds of antibiotics. But never enough infections in a row nor within a certain period of time to meet those blessed criteria for tubes. I asked often if she could get them. I mean, could one think of a better candidate for these tubes than a nonverbal two-year-old with a history of ear infections and fluid? Hindsight is so clear. The ENT kept saying she was not a candidate yet. It was so stressful. I wish I had been more assertive and more sure of myself at this time because knowing what I know now, I, for sure, would have acted and spoken so differently. This child needed to talk.

As a sidebar here, what also made this whole experience each and every month so difficult was that Elizabeth kept crying and screaming and fighting the doctor and nurses, as if she had never had an ear check before or had never seen these same people before. Sadly, they did begin to lose patience with her. They were tired of trying to calm her or, in many cases, restrain her. I was thankful at the time to have someone to check Elizabeth, but it was so hard, and I absolutely dreaded the moment I would peek into the waiting room and see it was full. Man, my anxiety started, and I would again almost sweat as I prayed to hear her name called. When they did finally call her name, she would scream or fight. It was simply stressful from start to finish.

Some time passed, and I asked again if and when she could get tubes, and that is when the trouble started. The doctor said she had not had fluid for three consecutive months and did not have enough ear infections documented to get tubes. . But she needed those tubes. She needed to hear. And she needed to be without pain. But I listened to him and just kept checking those ears again and again. Again, I need to say: advocate for your child. Be assertive.

About this same time, we started to investigate finding a speech pathologist to begin speech classes. We went to the local speech and language center for an evaluation. The testing went okay as they did not make her do anything, but they observed her and saw her inability to verbalize a word. It was at this time I received my first of what would be many looks of pity. I had seen them before on the faces of people in the store or the library, but not yet from a therapist who, I would have guessed, had seen a number of speech-delayed cases before. I was floored by the look, and I really did not know what to say. She did say that Elizabeth was a candidate for speech, something I had felt all along.

I left there feeling not so good. They did not seem to feel comfortable with Elizabeth and her crying and her refusal to touch anything. We were left in a quandary. But again I say God's hand was guiding us, as I overheard two moms talking about speech class that their kids were taking, and I was able to get the name of the therapist who treated children in her home. Kathy M. *Well now,* I thought, *do I call her and surprise her with Elizabeth at her doorstep, or tell her all about Elizabeth and then show up on her doorstep?* I decided to be fair and call her first.

I knew right away that she was *it* for us. I told her all about the crying and that Elizabeth was nonverbal, and that she did not like to touch things. Kathy said she would be happy to see us and work with Elizabeth. I would like to say that Kathy was an angel placed in our path. She loved our child from the first day and to this day, she still works with her. I consider Kathy one of my dearest friends, and I thank her for taking on this scared child way back when.

When Elizabeth was two-and-a-half years old, we had speech in line, and an ENT. I was just beginning to really understand the scope of how bad things were for this child. Initially, at Kathy's house, she began crying after only five minutes, and that ended what should have been a thirty-minute session. But Kathy was calm and said we would build from there. *But come on,* I told myself, *it was easy to rationalize the bad stuff when it was just me at home with Emily, but to put Elizabeth into the world and really look at her was horrible.* I did everything Kathy asked me to do with her to get Elizabeth to make any utterance. Kathy rewarded her with M&Ms® each time she made a sound, so I tried it, but I bought the ten-pound bag instead of the small one. And I thought, *There, now we will really get going.* I did everything that was asked. But the progress was so very slow.

Kathy practiced the kind of speech therapy called "whole language," so instead of sitting at a table and repeating words or sounds, she used conversational speech and had the child repeat key words that have the sounds in them that need to be worked on. She also had a theme for the week, such as birthday week. She talked about birthdays, and the kids would do a small activity with a birthday theme; they made a birthday treat and picked a prize. So in addition to the conversation, Elizabeth got exposed to activities and topics that were fun. I was happy that Kathy was exposing Elizabeth to such fun things and even though she resisted so much,

I was sure she was learning. Sometimes she lasted ten minutes into the session, and then the next session only two minutes. I would not dare to let myself look down the road we were on because I knew I really did not want to know.

It is funny, though, but I somehow knew she was learning things and that she was smart. I always believed there was so much more inside her than the child she was showing to the world. I am so thankful and happy that those feelings were inside me, because I have made many a decision with John about our next move for Elizabeth based on those deep-seated feelings. They have guided me and strengthened me through so much.

Life at home continued on in about the same way. We did things and had fun, but it was always with one eye on how we were going to get Elizabeth through it, whether it was the park, the library, or friends' houses. Every day was a push and a battle, but what was the option? We could stay home and listen to crying, or we could try to give her and Emily a happy life. After all, didn't Emily deserve a trip to the park or story time? I think back on this time and wonder how I did it. I think I was running on high all the time, kind of like on adrenaline all day long, as my anxiety was in high gear every day and night!

Oh! How Will We Do it All?

Elizabeth's ears had been somewhat evaluated, and she was now with a speech pathologist. And then we got the phone call from the O.T, fresh from her maternity leave. And here we go!

As I said before, I had made an initial phone call to Maureen. This is the call I had been waiting for. She and I talked for a good while about Elizabeth, and I can distinctly remember wishing she would say Elizabeth had a treatable problem, but at the same time almost wishing she didn't. No one really wants to know that their child has anything wrong with her. Isn't that funny? One would think I would be leaping at a chance to put a label on her. Anyway, we decided an evaluation was the next logical step for us. We scheduled it for the next week. And here is where I really think our journey in sensory processing disorder began.

The evaluation was scheduled for an afternoon in May. Elizabeth would be nearing her third birthday. She and I went into the therapy center, and I can still feel how nervous we were. It was such a beautiful spring day. But all I could think about was that I had no idea of what I was doing there or what was going to happen to her, or us, in this evaluation. Elizabeth was very scared, and Miss Maureen was extremely kind. She took us back to the therapy room, which was filled with toys and balls, blocks and mats. There were mirrors and dolls, and then in the one corner, there was a flat swing suspended from the ceiling, hanging over a mat. Near to it were other swings shaped like tubes or circles. I had never been to an occupational therapy setting before, so my eyes were taking it all in. Elizabeth was so scared, now she was shaking and holding on to me more than she had ever done before.

Maureen sat us down and tried to engage Elizabeth in a task of reaching into a pail filled with colored bean-bags and she cried, but Maureen did what I learned was a hand-over-hand method and "helped" Elizabeth do it. "Hand-over-hand method" means you hold the child's hand in yours and move their hand to do the task you wish done. In that way, they learn the way it feels to do a new task. So she did this for a while, and let me tell you, the tears never stopped; and if I even switched sitting positions, she jumped into my arms. I was sure her sensory system was in panic mode. After all, she was now being asked to do tasks, but it didn't stop like it would when we asked her to do things at home. Maureen, however, was holding her hand and guiding her, and so Elizabeth was not so easily able to cry her way out of the situation.

Maureen evaluated her and her ability to tolerate touching items, such as blocks, or sitting on a riding toy. All of this elicited arching of her back and crying. Maureen put her on the swing, and she loved going back and forth while on her tummy, but she would not reach for a beanbag placed just a bit ahead of her. As all this was going on, all I could see was a crying three-year-old. But to Maureen, she saw all the signs and characteristics of a child with sensory issues.

Children with sensory issues do not like to touch different textures or items. They do not like to move their bodies through different planes, kind of like if you got dizzy easily, you would stay nice and still and not turn your head or reach out to move yourself around much. Apparently Elizabeth liked to stay as still or as straight as possible so as not to disturb her vestibular system. Kids with SPD have a tough time judging where they are in space, meaning they find it comforting to keep two feet on the ground and their eyes straight ahead, but reaching out for something and having to balance themselves is hard and scary.

So now I was trying to comfort Elizabeth after nearly an hour of an evaluation and Maureen said that, in her opinion, Elizabeth showed all the signs of a child with SPD, and she suggested we meet again next week to do a little more of an evaluation and then begin treatments. So I agreed and went home and marked my calendar. We were on our way now. To where and how long it would take us to get there, I had no idea. But now we had two people on our team, and at least we were not alone.

The advice I would give at this point is twofold: one, please visit the website of the SPD Foundation, which specializes in the disorder, to get information sent to you; and two, find an occupational therapist in your town who has a background in SPD. Ours was located at the out-patient rehabilitation center of one of the local hospitals. It doesn't have to be someone affiliated with a hospital, a special needs school, or a program. Initally, I found someone who knew about the condition but was unable to help us, as we were not enrolled in their program.

Also, I suggest taking notes and taking the time to ask the therapists how or what you can do at home to follow up with the therapies. At first, I tried to remember them and then I would get confused and forget some. Later, I learned to write them down or asked the therapist to do it for me so that I could do them at home each week. And that is the other thing: following through at home is so, so important. I tried to do everything on the list each day. Imagine how much change you can affect, doing all that work each and every day instead of only once a week. I know it is hard to find the time to do these therapies, but they do make a world of difference when they are repeated daily. Of course, I knew I could not make a swing for her at home, but the other things could be done.

Also something to think about is to check one's insurance for coverage for OT treatments. Some companies will allow more sessions than others, and some may set a limit based on the child's age. When Elizabeth reached school age, our insurance company said they would be cutting our coverage because, in their eyes, she would now fall into the realm of our local school system. The school system and its programs were expected to take the place of outpatient therapy. Whew! What a lot of information. I know, but it is something I had to say, as I made a *huge* error early on with Elizabeth. When I think back on it, I absolutely cringe. But we initially had great OT coverage, and she was young enough not to red flag the insurance company's eyes.

But I actually opted to see the O.T. once every two weeks or even, *gulp*, once a month. I reasoned we could do the follow-up at home more consistently if I did not have to change our "homework" every week. What a mistake! I was soon to see was that we had so much to do with, and for, Elizabeth that we would constantly be changing what we did. I should've jumped at the chance to have O.T. sessions as often as possible.

And here is one huge thing to know, that as you do these therapies, things will get worse before they get better. In other words, the therapies themselves are so stressful for the child and their system that Elizabeth would be upset or scared, and I would wonder if I should stop pushing her to do this new thing. But then after a few tries or days, she would accomplish the task, and then I would be so happy and proud and motivated to do more.

Now back to our second visit to the O.T. I can remember that when we arrived, I took a good look at the place and I saw some people who I assumed were parents or caregivers in the waiting room, and they were very relaxed and having the requisite Styrofoam cup of coffee, watching TV. I wondered how could they be so okay sitting there and even more, how could their child be alone in therapy and not be crying? Would that ever be me? Would we ever get to that point? Only time would tell.

So we got back into the room, and Maureen began to assess Elizabeth as she touched items, such as foamy soap or sand or even chalk. Of course she always cried and cringed and, of course, I had to be there by her side and even be the first one to touch the item, as if to tell Elizabeth everything would be okay if Mom survived touching it.

At the conclusion of the hour, Maureen definitely gave the opinion that Elizabeth had sensory integration dysfunction and that she would like to see her as many times as possible starting soon. I remember telling Maureen that we had our first family vacation scheduled for the next week; we were going to the beach and that we could start treatments in three weeks. Maureen said that either Elizabeth would love the beach or she would hate it, and if the latter happened, I was to swing her in a towel, as if she were in a hammock. To calm her system, I was instructed to do something called "body brushing." This required me to use a small brush like the doctors used for cleaning before a surgery. I was to brush her arms and legs and her back ten times each to calm her.

Maureen mentioned one other thing called "propriocep-tive input." This is the calm feeling one gets after a weight-lifting workout, due to the input of the weight bearing on the joints. I was told something called "joint compressions" could achieve a degree of this calmness, and I was quickly taught how to do them for Elizabeth. Maureen wished us good luck and said she would see us in three weeks.

I remember packing for this first trip and remember-ing what Maureen said to help me help Elizabeth cope with the trip. By the way, did I mention we were *driv-ing* the fourteen-plus hours hour trip to Myrtle Beach? Seriously, what were John and I thinking?

I will simply say that I did the things Maureen sug-gested, and they helped. I let her bounce on the bed, as that created the proprioceptive calm and gave her some joint compressions that are part of the sensory diet, the term used for all the things one does each day for a child like Elizabeth. These joint compressions send a calming message to her neurological system and help her. I also did body brushing. This is to help her system to relax and allow the input of sensory information. Both these components are supposed to calm the child, and thereby decrease their defensiveness and its resulting anxiety.

Well, I did those things as we traveled. She jumped up and down at rest stops, and I brushed her often but not sooner than every two hours, as that is how long the effects last. And she really did a good job of traveling. We had some difficulty in the new bathrooms or at the hotel with the new crib and room. But we did it! We took the chance and made it to the beach. I cannot put into words the way I felt being there. It was so liberating, and I could breathe. The world was really still out there. We had been in our world, encapsulated for so long that to see this beautiful, wonderful place almost made me cry. To see other people laughing and having fun was great. I could almost let go for a small moment. I actually walked on the beach that first night by myself and thought, *Thank you, God, for your strength and for letting us be here. Thank you for this success. Thank you for this time we have to enjoy together.*

And, much to our happy surprise, Elizabeth and the beach became the best of friends. The ocean, its waves, and its rhythm calmed her. She loved the ocean then and adores it to this day. I still had to be with her at all times and in her field of vision, but we did it. We were on vacation! Emily had a great vacation too! She loved it all.

I love those memories. Wow, the simple joys are so great sometimes. This was something that this journey with Elizabeth has taught us. The simple things are the best. Love every day, every success, and each other, as much as you can. God gave us these challenges and through them, the good things were so magnified that a simple walk on the beach to others was okay, but to us it was the most amazing gift. Our family still lives that way today. You will find us laughing over ice cream or being the first family on the street to play in the new snow. Each and every little thing and gift of time and love does not go unappreciated. That is one of the gifts of our Elizabeth.

Finally We Meet Our Mary!

We began our O.T. treatments when we got back home, and we still had our speech therapy scheduled each week. I will say our days took on new form for sure. As I said, I would get the "homework" from both Kathy and Maureen, and then ask myself how I could accomplish these things at home. What was great for me was that Emily was always willing to do these activities. I tried to make them fun instead of therapy-like, and Emily would love them. Usually I could get Elizabeth to try things, usually for very short times, but I would take any success at this point. I reasoned these successes were from doing what a professional instructed, so I knew we were headed in the right direction.

I think now is the time to tell you a little about this big sister, Emily. She is only two and one half years older than Elizabeth, but it always seemed she was older. Even to talk to Emily, one just seemed to know she understood things, so no one talked to her like she was too little to understand. And it seemed like that was the case from day one. Emily is the perfect sister for Elizabeth and has never once let her down. She loved her from the start, and to this day she is the one Elizabeth goes to for hugs. When I get upset with her, she seeks out Emily.

People don't always realize just what it is like to be the sister of a special needs child, and Emily never once wished for her sister to be anyone or anything other than who she is. I think I am failing Emily here trying to describe her, but she is a child with a golden, loving heart, and we are more proud of her than we could ever say in this book or the next. God put these two sisters together, and they simply love one another.

From what I have read, many times the "typical" developing sibling can feel left out or underappreciated due to the attention garnered by the child in need. But such is not the case in our family. John and I always made time for Emily, and we always praised her hard work at school or art or any endeavor. I am glad God guided us in this path, because I would hate to think that we would have seen successes for Elizabeth while having sacrificed Emily in the process. I suggest for anyone on a journey with a special needs child: make time to see and talk to the siblings. They need to vent and have time with you. And see them and their daily events, really see them.

It was always so wonderful to spend time talking to Emily each day. She made my heart smile on days when not much else did. I began to let Emily skip her naps so I could make sure to spend two to three hours each day while Elizabeth slept just being with her to play and focus on her. It was exhausting to go all day, but it was so, so worth it. Being a stay-at-home mom, the days can blend one into another so much that those high points were treasured. So Emily and Elizabeth and I did these exercises from Maureen each day. They were tough and such hard work for Elizabeth, but I knew I had to push her and push her to keep accomplishing things. I never, not once at any point, felt she could not do something. I just felt it was a matter of practice and believing.

It was about now in her life that I began telling her that I believed in her. I would lie with her each night after reading our books and say, "I know you can do anything in this world because I believe in you." I said it each night, and to this very day, I say it and she finishes the sentence for me. She knows how we feel about her and how much we love her. I told her that I push her because I know she can do it. I knew if I let certain feelings in, I would feel bad for Elizabeth and I would not be strong, so I did not allow those feelings in. Once in a while, those feelings snuck in, and I would just cry and cry for the life this child was missing and all the work she had to do each day. I could not believe all she had yet to learn and do. But I just knew there was so much more inside of her than she was showing.

In a weird way, I decided I would not treat her differently from Emily. I thought if Emily had to listen and try, so did Elizabeth. As she made gains later in life, I insisted on manners and jobs for her, just like Emily. I wanted her to know that we did not pity her and that she was one of us, not an entity unto her own. I know that setting this attitude early on was a huge plus for us. Then there were no questions concerning how we were to treat her. We believed in her, and we did not pity her. No way! She was going to grow and live, and that was that.

Those exercises from Maureen included placing Elizabeth on her tummy and making her reach for a stuffed animal in front of her (for Maureen, it was colored beanbags, but any port in a storm, they say). We did speech work together and, for the record, Emily and I polished off the reward bag of M&Ms® pretty quickly. But boy, was it a lot of work every day. I would record activities on the papers, and what kind of success or failures we had. I recommend doing lots of recordkeeping. It was so I could start where we left off the next day, no sense in repeating what we had already succeeded in, after all. I was, and still am, looking for the next thing to do for her.

So that is the life now, home with my two girls, Elizabeth, about three and a half years old and Emily, five, and my husband who has a very busy internal medicine practice, with late hours and plenty of on-call nights. I tried to keep our home calm, and it was hard work. But we had a daily schedule and now a therapy schedule, and I found that the schedule was as comforting to me as it was to the kids. I made sure to have some downtime each night for John and I to talk and relax and to ready ourselves for the next day.

One thing I highly recommend is time to yourself to do something each day, to treat yourself, even if it is as simple as a special cup of coffee or a new book. For me, it was my exercise routine. I did something physical each day, and it helped me mentally more than I can say. I still work out daily and during stressful times for us, I find I look forward to it. I can remember after so many mornings as we just survived, I literally couldn't wait to dive on the treadmill and just lose myself in a movie or a show. I know I hated to come up the steps to my world so much that I wished I could have been adopted by the *Sopranos* family, or at least become the fifth friend in *Sex and the City*.

We, as a family, were definitely in a situation that was ours alone. Everyone had kids that were just humming along, and we did not. I am so thankful that we were the kind of family we are, because I could see how a special needs child could split a family or a marriage. The stress is with you every day all day. John was my first love, and we married after dating only each other. He is my best friend and my touchstone. I cannot thank him enough for being who he was and is in all situations. He is a wonderful, loving, open father and husband, the kind who hugs us all the time. Simply put, he loves completely. We definitely have our base of love and faith to help us.

With John's hours so long and unpredictable, it was hard to get Elizabeth to the appointments and somehow still make it fun for Emily. I was always so aware of trying to keep Emily's world as normal as I could, and this is where I am so happy that the outpatient O.T. facility was located near my mom and dad's house. My kids call them "Mimi" and "Popi." My kids love them so much, and always have such fun and get such love from them. You know that wonderful, unconditional kind of love? Well, it comes in great amounts from them. My mom and dad were always willing to babysit our kids, and they still are. So blessed are my children to have them. I would drop Emily off at their house, and then Elizabeth and I would trot off to therapy.

I grew to become quite friendly with the staff at the center, and they grew to understand Elizabeth and all her unique ways. As we made gains, Maureen would tell me that Elizabeth was doing better this time, or look, she tried to reach for this bean bag, or she was happy she could place her on the swing and move it in a different direction than last time. I was present at all the therapies, and I had to actually do the therapies first, so I was climbing on swings and touching foamy soap, coloring or cutting.

I remember Maureen telling me, "One day, Michele, you will be sitting out in the waiting room, I promise."

And I know I kind of smiled and thought, *I really do not believe you.*

I met a wonderful lady there named Carmel. She actually worked at the center, and we became friends.

She was always smiling and always patient and kind to Elizabeth. In fact, it was Carmel who was the first person other than my mom and dad to watch our children. She let me see that someone else could become a part of our world and that we could relax a bit, and for that we are always so thankful to her.

I wish I had known how slow the progress would be, and I guess that is an important thing to know ahead of time. It takes a great deal of appointments and follow-through at home to see changes. I know that I kept waiting for the one new thing they would try that would magically fix Elizabeth, like swinging to the left would make her lose this sensory problem. I was naïve to think that it would go away. I learned that it abates, but it will never leave her.

In terms of her dyspraxia, Maureen would work on any fine motor skills she could, like holding a pencil, cutting, playing with Silly Putty®, or stringing beads. Her gross motor skills were being worked on at the same time she was swinging or hopping or reaching for items. The treatment addressed both the problems.

One thing that did not change was her ear infections or ear problems. I was still on the hunt for those tubes, and still we were denied them by the ENT. I recommend advocating and investigating options for your child if that still, quiet voice inside of you tells you to do something. Why didn't I take her to another ENT for a second opinion? Well, I can't change what I did not do, but something happened this fall/winter of her life that was the most important thing for Elizabeth and her future.

Elizabeth's godmother, Denise, went to a continuing education course for her speech-pathology license and attended a seminar given by Mary P. It turns out she specialized in sensory processing disorder and dyspraxia, and was a speech pathologist! Her caseload consisted of children who had multi-sensory processing disorders, which involved a spectrum of diagnoses that included dyspraxia, apraxia, autism spectrum disorders, sensory processing disorders, and genetic disorders that resulted in the above mentioned. She was perfect for us, and she was only one hour away from our home.

Officially, Mary has the following initials after her name "MA,CCC/SLP." She has a master's of arts in communication disorders, with a specialty in multi-sensory processing disorders. She also possesses a certificate of Clinical Competence and licensure in Speech Language Pathology. I thank God for placing Denise in this course and Mary in our path.

I called her right away. What a phone call that one was! I remember keeping her on the phone close to two solid hours, me talking and Mary asking for more information. I have never felt so unburdened when it came to Elizabeth as I did that very night. I poured out my heart and soul to this lady I did not know at all, and she was wonderful. I followed up the phone call with an e-mail, answering some of the questions Mary had asked me. She also gave me an overview of her philosophies and beliefs, pertaining to how she does her therapies. Here is her explanation of SPD and her goals from an e-mail posted in October of 2000.

> Thank you for your inquiry based on the talk heard on the tenth. I would be happy to see Elizabeth for an evaluation, but maybe I should give you some of my philosophies toward evaluation and treatment first to see if you're still interested. I do not use standardized assessment, particularly for a child of this young age. My assessment is based on normal sensory motor development and its relationship to language, speech and communication development. I feel very strongly about nutrition and its effect on brain processing, so I would be interested in Elizabeth's diet and whether or not she has any known food allergies. I take a holistic approach to therapy, looking at all factors that could be inhibiting or enhancing a child's growth and development. I believe in alternative medicine and alternative therapies, used in conjunction with solid behavioral and sensory based therapy…it is this holistic approach that allows the child to make the most rapid gains. I would think that if you've been able to pull off some form of sensory diet (Miss Maureen's), hopefully between the two of us, and any significant others involved, we'll be able to draw a strong, intensive, sensory diet to the benefit of Elizabeth.

Wow, quite a lot of words for sure, but to think of a person who is looking at all parts of Elizabeth and somehow putting all the pieces together. Yes, please! To those who are reading this and want to find someone who would approach your child in this fashion, I recommend calling the SPD Foundation for any recommendation they can make. Their phone number is (303) 794–1182, or go to their website: www.spdfoundation.net. For information regarding dyspraxia, you can call (773)248–3476 or please visit the *Dyspraxia USA* website: www.dyspraxiausa.org.

Also, remember that even if you have been given a name of a therapist, I have been told by Mary for the purpose of this book that one should actually interview the therapist regarding their methods, beliefs, and goals. It is really okay to ask the important questions, as this person will be working with your child. And as a matter of record, I never interviewed someone. It actually never occurred to me to do this. I usually asked about the therapist and their reputation and demeanor, but that is all. So I hope this piece of information helps others because maybe if I would have done that, I would not have made so many twists and turns in our journey.

We booked our evaluation with Mary as soon as possible. John took the day off, Emily went to my mom's, and off we went. The evaluation was so long, so informative, so overwhelming, and so great, and way too much information for me to handle. I came home with seven pages, front and back, filled with homework, as I like to say, to help Elizabeth. We had a new brushing protocol every two hours, with joint compressions also every two hours. I learned the correct way to brush her. Up and down, ten times per arm and leg, then her back but never her tummy, using enough pressure to bend the bristles of the brush for the best results. The joint compressions consist of holding the shoulder with one hand and kind of pushing the upper arm toward the shoulder with the other ten times, then moving to the lower arm and then to each finger, always pushing the joints into one another gently but firmly. Then she was to jump ten times to stimulate her legs. And this was every two hours every day for months and months. According to Mary, this would keep her system in a place of balance and allow her to relax and input sensory information, and do some of the other one million things on earlier pages.

I thought we had a sensory diet before. Ha-ha, I laugh at that one. *This* diet was huge and all encompassing. We did mouth work for her lack of speech, as she was still nonverbal at this point. Crying was her only communication. We did blowing exercises and oral exploration with a nux brush, the little rubber brush used to clean a baby's gums. We used it to stimulate Elizabeth's mouth. I used that brush to stroke the inside of her cheeks and the roof of her mouth.

Mary wanted us to do pillow wrestling and lotion rubs. She wanted us to work on getting Elizabeth to move the trunk as she kept her body in a straight line. For her balance, she wanted us to have her lay on an exercise ball on her tummy, and extend her arms. I was to put her in a blanket and slowly swing her and to encourage playing on a playground. We also did balance exercises where she sat on an exercise ball and pretended to row on each side.

As you can see, this was all hard stuff for us to do together. It was all new to Elizabeth and all new to her system. There were plenty of tears and screaming for sure (I am not sure if it was more her than me at times), and it took so much time to accomplish these things every day, especially with the brushing being done every two hours.

I wanted so much to do all of this stuff and still keep Emily happy. So because Emily was not yet in any school, we just did these things all together. Emily would do the activity first, then Elizabeth would scream and cry and try to do something. And on and on we went. Each day we did this, and I would record the progress and/or number of attempts we were able to accomplish. Wow, even as I write this, I feel myself reliving some of those moments, and I am almost instantly tired. But we did it, and Elizabeth achieved success in doing these things.

I kept Mary up-to-date with frequent e-mails, and then we had another session with her in March of 2001. In my journal I wrote that on this session, Mary just increased the demands of all the areas we were already working in, such as more times doing each one, and we kept on with the brushing. She did add "thinking language" to the mix, which meant asking questions to Elizabeth to help her think of an answer. No more yes or no questions to her.

Wow, what a year. And wow, what a great person Mary was for us. I quickly learned that we were making headway and achieving our goals, and so everything we did was with a purpose. I put myself in the mindset that every activity, be it Mary's idea or just an everyday one, became a chance for me to incorporate some sensory or motor issues for Elizabeth. Whether it was marching in place or playing with foamy soap in the tub or even tossing pillows, everything was done with a purpose. Once you get in this mindset, the therapy becomes almost second nature to you and the household, which I think is a good thing.

Mary and I also e-mailed each other often and as I reread some of them, I am so thankful for how far we have come. I cannot believe how much we have done in all these years. Something else we did to keep the communications current was for me to make a videotape of Elizabeth as she and I would be doing the activities of her sensory diet, or her gross motor work. This way Mary could see her and her reactions, positions, and responses, and then offer her suggestions. It was so much easier than for me to try to describe to Mary how Elizabeth reacted. Seeing firsthand definitely was the best. Mary would always offer her ideas and thoughts related to my e-mails and videos.

The work was hard and constant, but one thing I suggest is taking the time to digest the new information given to you, and try to figure out a way to put the new exercises and items into your day. I know I initially would feel so overwhelmed and was just so sure that I could not fit one more thing into our day. Then I would let the new information settle in and I would look at it after a bit, and it would then seem more manageable. I know how hard I would try to get in as many of Mary's ideas as possible each day. After a while, it just became part of my day to do these sensory things and to do these oral or gross motor exercises.

I will offer one more piece of advice. As much as I say I wanted to do so much each day, it is important to know you cannot do them all. Early on, I nearly made myself crazy in my attempts to follow the instructions to the T. Give yourself a break. I would soon be told this is definitely a marathon and not a sprint.

So every day, as we did the sensory diet as prescribed, we then went about our day as best we could, sneaking in more things as Elizabeth's system would allow. We did this to benefit the sensory issues as well as the dyspraxic part of her diagnosis. I will say I did see a change in her. She appeared calmer, and she did try things a little bit before the tears and crying started. So things were going in the right direction.

We give to Mary the biggest thanks we can for all of her guiding and caring for us during those first few treatments. We really were a group in need, and I hung on her every word. If she would have told me to paint myself purple and stand on my head, I guarantee you would've found me purple and upside down. That is how much

I trusted and still trust her. Mary is a dear, wonderful, brilliant friend, and we still see her but instead of every month or so, we are down to one tune-up time a year; and this year, we did not go at all.

I do need to be truthful, so I will admit that I call her close to once a week to check in about something or to ask her opinion of something. But the homework from her has ceased to come to us in a full ream of paper. To see how far we have come, I think back to this time, then I look up to the mud puddle that Elizabeth and her brother, Michael, are jumping in today. Yes, we have we come a long way. Elizabeth is now near to four years old. What a road it has been.

She's Going to Preschool

It is amazing to think Elizabeth will be four years old soon. In the past year, she has been seen by so many people, more therapists than many people will see in a lifetime. I do see changes in her moods and demeanor. I wrote in her journal that I have kept from birth "that she is using more and more words ... that she plays all day and is gaining her equilibrium or balance." I wrote that her schedule at this point is Tuesday at Kathy's, Thursday at O.T., and one time a month for a visit to Mary. So we are busy, but she is making gains, and I love it.

I think the hardest part of dealing with Elizabeth is that outwardly she is absolutely beautiful and has these huge, blue eyes. She, for the most part, appears as if nothing is wrong with her. Then someone will approach her, and I see the same scenario unfold each time. She can't answer their greeting, she pulls away or will cry if touched, and then I will apologize and say the old, "She's tired, sorry."

I hated it all. I hated the stares. I hated that once someone saw anything amiss in her, they would talk down to her. I was starting to feel the effects of all this stress from Elizabeth. She was out in the world so much more, and I was just so nervous everywhere. I felt like I was walking forward with my arms reaching back, as if to protect her from the world of stares and comments; I was always running interference for her, and it was exhausting and really futile because you cannot anticipate all things, and something would always occur that was unexpected.

It was like I could not wait to get out of any social situations in which she or I would or could be looked at. I so hated the stares and judgmental looks, that I wanted to be in and out of places before anyone could have the time to notice her. And for the record, one cannot achieve this goal no matter how hard you try, and believe me I have tried. I had to tell myself so many times, *You are okay, you are almost done.* Over and over until I really was done.

And again, for the record, I hated this too! I was surprised at how much I began to hate, and feel nervous, and wanted to cry. And all this from a person who was previously pretty optimistic. I really was losing myself bit by bit, and all in the pursuit of finding my daughter. I had to push so hard each day.

And then here was my little Emily. She needed a mom who was strong and fun and happy. So I pretended for her. And I did it each day. I would hold my heart together as it got crushed each time I saw other moms with typical kids. I wanted that so badly, and I never got it. But outwardly, I looked great. Inside, I did not know me at all anymore.

I started to live for the small gains Elizabeth would make. I would be so happy when she did something new or showed any interest in anything new. I remember that when she started to like certain things, like sprinkles on her cookies, and wearing bracelets, I always got so excited that I would want to go out and buy fifteen of those things. And I would almost want to say to anyone, "See, look at those bracelets, isn't it something to see her like these things?" To others with typically developing kids, they would just put the bracelets out for their kids and would not see the big deal in it.

There is one heartbreaking, and yet in a way beautiful, story that shows the world what this child could feel and understand. I remember going to the store with my mom and Elizabeth. Elizabeth was in a pair of shorts and a T-shirt, and I remember my mom taking her into the back of the store and showing her dresses and matching socks. Well, much to my surprise, I looked to see that my mom had changed Elizabeth into a pretty dress and a pair of socks while they were in the store and not in a changing room. I am sure she did it that way to keep Elizabeth relaxed. So my mom buys this outfit for Elizabeth and she wears it home. She seems so happy with the outfit and, of course, she was not yet able to verbalize this to us.

Well that night, I put the dress in her closet and tucked her in. As I went to bed, I peeked into her room as I always did to check her and Emily, and I could not find her. She was not in her bed. She was not next to it. So I kind of panicked, and then I saw that the closet was still lit. Well, much to my astonishment, I found her sleeping on the floor of the closet, hugging her new dress and socks. I almost cried for her and how much the new dress meant to her. She actually got up out of bed while thinking of the dress and took it off the hanger and lay down with it. All those things she did alone and because she wanted to. If I needed something more to make me so sure of her feelings and abilities, that was it. She *is* with us and she *does* feel and value things. I took a mental picture of her with that dress and I look at it often, and it tells me so much about my lovely, sweet child.

Our time with Mary this year finds her telling us that we need to work on making facial expressions with Elizabeth and to focus on teaching her what they mean and how to try to make them, such as happy or sad. (Yes, we really did have to teach a lot of things.) Because Elizabeth could never relax enough to let information in, so much needed to be taught. We also were told to make an obstacle course in the basement to have Elizabeth work her muscles and motor planning to transition from one activity to another. So I did it. It had six stations like hanging on a bar, then pushing a scooter on hands and knees, then walking on our balance beam, doing the walk on hands and feet, bent over. And we did it three or four times. And we had our fair share of crying over this one, let me tell you. But again, she did it. It was not easy, but she did it.

All I can think about is how very much we love her and how much we want her to keep growing and achieving. Every night I say those words to her, "I believe in you." And every night, I thank God she is coming out of her world of fear and beginning to feel calm.

Can you imagine for a minute being near what you fear the most, and no one is making it go away for you? I imagine this is what she felt like having to see, hear, and feel things. I am unable to tell you how brave I feel this little girl is, and I pray at this point God's will includes her growing each day.

As for her language, we were seeing Elizabeth make some progress. She was saying words her way, meaning not quite whole words but more like half words. She would leave off the end sounds. She was making gains in her gross motor play, that is for sure. She began to like seeing people, and she would try to engage the kids who were waiting to go next at Kathy's. She said hi to them and kind of followed them, not in a completely inappropriate way, just near to them as they walked to Kathy. I don't know if I encouraged her in her pursuit, or if I was feeling protective of her in this situation, but I do know that I was seeing her eyes being so bright and lively, not so scared all of the time. It is absolutely heartbreaking to see your child look terrified of things that are really not scary to most people. Having seen that look in her those eyes before, I love, love, love seeing those bright baby blues.

Kathy was very encouraging of this behavior and kept telling me that Elizabeth was a very social child. My first thought was, *Really? My little Elizabeth, the one who really can't talk and hides from many things?* But I kept hearing this over and over again from Kathy, and she said that she thinks Elizabeth needed her own social group. Well for me, of course, I am so busy with my day-to-day life that I would not have begun to think of this turn of events. "Seriously? A school for this little wonder?" But I trusted Kathy so much, that I took her advice to look into a special preschool. A preschool that was in some way tied to our local system. We would need to go through an evaluation and testing to qualify.

Before I tell about this preschool and the testing itself, I feel I need to say that it so important to be educated about a new school or therapy or therapist. I learned this the hard way. Had I known that the school would start an IEP, or Individualized Education Plan, based on this testing for preschool entrance that would indeed follow Elizabeth for years and put us in the focus of the school system's special education office sooner than I would have liked, I know I would have passed up this opportunity. I was not at all ready to put her on some education track based on this initial testing. I mean, she had only been in therapy for one year at the time. I felt she would be growing so much more and that we had two more years or so before we had to present our situation to the school. I will say that that IEP followed us for the next two years, even after we had left the preschool. I am not saying our child did not need services or did not have special needs;

I am saying we were working so hard for her gains, that to set her on a path this early based on these tests was unfair to her. Please make yourself aware of what future consequences your current action may have.

It was hard to get the special education team to understand us when we described Elizabeth's ways to them. It was equally hard for them to understand me. I know I came off as very defensive and protective of Elizabeth, as I was both those things. But then again, I deserved to be such. I had been in this fight for four years by then, and I felt my opinion counted. And I am sure I offended some of the educators when I was so insistent on things being my way. But I am happy I was a good advocate for Elizabeth. I really wasn't trying to be difficult at the time. I was just trying to make sure everything was in order for our child.

I advise those looking at a preschool to ask the questions I did not ask. Will there be an IEP? And if so, make sure that the initial narrative explanation of your child is to your liking, with all the information you need in there. And remember, the IEP is a fluid document. You can change it when you want to by calling a meeting with the special education team. I did not know any of this at the time, and initially, I signed where they asked me to and I did what they said, and I entered her into a school that she would ultimately stay in for only three months.

This preschool had 50 percent special needs kids and 50 percent typically developing kids. I was told that prior to getting into the school, Elizabeth would have to go through an assessment called PAINT, otherwise known as preschool multifactored evaluation. This assessment would be play-based and would have many components. The evaluators would be looking at social interactions, language, gross and fine motor skills, and adaptive behaviors. Elizabeth and many others were to play as these educators watched and asked us questions. Based on their observances, an evaluation was made. Well, one can guess based on Elizabeth's history, play has not been her strong point, so she did very little for them. She could not draw a face, cut or color, voluntarily stack blocks, or feed a baby doll. She did not jump well or catch a ball.

The whole process was tough. Tough because, on one hand, I wanted her to do these things and show the world there was more to her than they thought and, on the other hand, I knew doing too much would make her ineligible for the program, and wasn't getting in the goal after all? Well, I need not have worried about her not getting in. The results showed she tested at the level of a nineteen-month-old child. *Nineteen months* and she was near to four years old; I could not believe how I was shaken by this result. I mean, I knew she was delayed due to her disorders, but this was more than I was ready for. And of course, she got in.

The evaluators told me she had plenty of splinter skills. That means some skills were higher on the developmental scale and some were lower. But as they watched her, if she missed or did not try to do two things in a row on their long list of things, that was considered her developmental age in the category they were testing. So, for example, if she could climb the steps right foot then left foot but couldn't bounce a ball or catch one, it didn't matter that the climbing was a more advanced skill. Those two misses would determine her developmental age in the gross motor area.

And it worked this way in every category. So I was completely devastated; I can remember being in a denial state and telling these testers of the things she could do. I mean, after all, we had been doing things, new tasks and hard tasks, with Maureen and Mary and Kathy, right? So I was so sad. They said Elizabeth had to do these skills by herself in order to count them as successes. And even though I knew that she needed a degree of help or guidance, I still felt she deserved some credit. But the evaluators did not.

I think that day was the biggest turning point for me; I told you how I just knew there was more inside of her. I had seen her learning and growing with her current treatments, and I knew she was so much smarter than she showed the world. But now I knew it was true. She was testing horribly because the test did not give her credit for the way *she* did things, for the fact that she needs a little more help to get going or that she may need two tries at something, not just one.

And that is the fight to this day. *She does things differently, not wrongly.* Elizabeth's way may not be the way the world does something, but she still does the task. It may take her more tries to learn something or more verbal cues, or a bit of assistance, but she can do things. I cannot tell you how many times I have stood up for her to many people who doubted her ability to learn. And as I explained her ways to them, I knew that so many times people would just look at me and smile at me as if to say I was living in my own world. Even though I have received my fair share of these looks, I never lost my resolve to advocate for her and push for her to be understood and helped.

It was now the fall of 2001, and I will say that in theory, I was glad she was going to be headed to school. I mean, she was going to go to a school that was to meet her needs with speech, and O.T. to be done daily. We had a big meeting to sign Elizabeth's IEP. This IEP outlined what needs she had and the plans to meet these needs. She had a great deal of needs, let me tell you. And one ongoing one was her ears.

I still believed that she needed to hear all the time, not sporadically, to make as many gains in her speech as possible. I could see her fragile speech gains go away when she had fluid in her ears or an ear infection. I would hear her few "words" become mumbled and would take her in for a checkup to be told she had fluid or an infection. So she would be treated and rechecked. I still could not believe she would not get those tubes. But that battle, since it was so ongoing, was fought on an as-needed basis. We were now on a new road in her first preschool.

School began for Elizabeth in early September of 2001. I remember taking pictures of Emily going into first grade and then trying to take a picture of Elizabeth for her first day of school ... ever. And all I could get was one of her crying. She hated having her picture taken. The preschool may meet the needs of some of the children, but it just seemed off for Elizabeth and her needs even from day one. I really can't explain why; it was just a feeling I had.

I honestly thought she would do well with just typically developing kids, not special needs kids, even though apparently we qualified as special needs ourselves. I had hoped she would learn as she watched the typical developing kids as I know she did watching Emily, Kathy, or Maureen. We were told that she would get both speech and O.T. daily and that she would learn how to function in a school, with a locker and rules and schedules. So in theory, it seemed okay. But in actuality, Elizabeth picked up the behaviors of the special needs kids and not those of the typical developing kids. After all, it was easier for her to yell or moan than color or talk. So I had a worse feeling after only one week at this school.

I did not relay these feelings I had to the teachers, for fear that they would take offense at the idea that we did not belong there. But I knew in my heart that we did not. True, I did not know exactly where we belonged, but I was just so sure it was not there.

I got a firsthand look at all parts of Elizabeth's day because I may have left out that I, too, went to preschool! I had to go each day so that she would go. I went each time she went for the first week; then I tried to taper it off by leaving the room a little at a time, if allowed, to see how she did. But I always stayed in the facility.

The preschool was housed in our local career and technical school. I know that it was against most normal ways to have the mom of a student be there, but I had to do things my way, and I will advocate to others to try to get the places you pick to work with you and your concerns.

I know I would have been incapable of just leaving her. Leaving a nonverbal child with sensory issues alone was just way out of my comfort zone. Just how could that have worked? I needed to tell them how she did things and how to understand her and her ways. I am happy to say that even though I had such unease about the fit of the preschool, Elizabeth was following the rules of the school and following the schedules of the day. She hung her coat in her locker, and I will say that the good of this experience was in the gift of seeing her abilities to do what was asked. She was coming out more and more. I was proud of her listening and her new skills.

I think what is hardest for me now is that I was so busy doing the therapies and following up at home and maintaining my day-to-day routine with Emily, that teaching Elizabeth how to put a coat on a hook or stand in line were not on my list of things to do; so I was always so pleasantly surprised and happy that someone else taught her something new.

As I mentioned, Elizabeth is a visual learner, so she learns best by watching, due in part to two reasons. The first being the ear infections and fluid in her ears that has sadly become so chronic for her, and as a result it has affected her hearing. The second reason is called an auditory processing disorder. We started on a venture with

Mary using The Listening Program, or TLP™, a music-based auditory retraining that focuses on improving the brain's understanding of what it hears. This is actually what auditory processing is. Auditory perception is measured and produced in "hertz," which is the frequency rate at which that sound is perceived and received to ultimately stimulate various parts of the brain, affecting mind and body balance. This program is like an intensive exercise program for the brain. There are thousands of nerve receptors that range in the frequency reception from 20hz-20khz. Elizabeth's processing disorder makes hearing and following through with ideas and requests hard for her. The words we *say* aren't received in the same way they are *said*, so following verbal directives is very difficult when someone has this disorder. Add in the anxiety she feels with something new and top it with dyspraxia and my, my, what a difficult scenario it is!

There is a special therapy that helps with this processing disorder. Mary guided us to this special music program that is used to retrain the brain to help with sound processing. I will tell you about it when Elizabeth turns five years old, as this was when we began it for her.

Being a visual learner means Elizabeth watches things so much and learns better with visual aids like demonstrations shown to her, or perhaps something that is manipulated in front of her to teach her. She will always do better this way rather than if someone just tells her something, reading the instructions off of a page to her. We all learn in a different way and prepare for tests or deadlines in our own way. I prepared for tests three days or more ahead of time, and my husband is a firm believer that one's best studying is done the night before a test.

The difference with Elizabeth is that she couldn't tell us at this point what she was able to learn or when she was feeling overwhelmed by words or commands. She would show these feelings by shutting down, crying, or throwing her head back and pulling away from any attempt to touch her or guide her to a new task. So there was always a shut-down time for her, and if she got to that point, it was bad and I was afraid they might not know what to do when she acted this way.

I wanted to teach them how to see the signs of her anxiety and impending melt-down, and then tell them some of the ways to calm her. These calming activities came from Mary and would be Elizabeth's sensory diet, tailored to a school day and its activities. I would consult with Mary via phone or e-mail and then relay the ideas to the preschool staff. Then I would watch to see if they were able to implement them or not. I had a lot of watching and talking and relaying of information to do. It was a busy time for me.

When someone new was working with Elizabeth, be it a new aide or a student helper, I had to tell them her unique ways and how to respond to her ways. I can tell you that it is a lot of work to do these things. I can see that the easiest path would have been to just let the staff do their day with her, and then I would pick her up at two o'clock. But that scenario just didn't work for me. I cannot stress enough how important it is to have all people who work with your child on the same page, working toward the same goals. I know the people in the preschool setting were trying hard for Elizabeth, so I really could not fault them in all their efforts, but I could not help but watch and wonder if they believed what I told them about her and all of the abilities I insisted she had. I was concerned that they were basing their actions on the original testing that got her into this school in the first place. In other words, was she a child capable of learning and achieving things in her own way, or was she a four-year-old with a developmental age of nineteen months? And I was a mother who needed a serious reality check? That dilemma kept me on my toes for sure.

We kept Elizabeth in the preschool for three months, and in those three months, she picked up a number of untoward behaviors, noisemaking and weird movements. I will say I did not see many other gains made other than her ability to go to the school without me present. That happened in the second month. As I said before, everything happens for a reason, and some good does come of all things; and of this situation, I will say the good is that I learned to be cautious of promises made by schools and professionals. I know therapists and other professionals have the best interests of the child at heart but as a mom and advocate, you need to watch your child's progress and not be afraid to ask questions or call for meetings and assert yourself. Remember, it is your child's life, and time and opportunities pass that you cannot get back.

I recommend really researching the environment you will be placing your child in and even talking to the people who may have attended the place. I did neither of these two things, as I was new to this process and, at this point, I was really listening to Kathy.

And Kathy was correct. To this day, Elizabeth loves to be with kids and grownups alike. She loves people and will even say as much to me. But I know I made a misstep here because of the behaviors she was learning and the smile face on a stick story.

The story goes a little something like this. Elizabeth is pretty much nonverbal. Yes, she says some words, but they are said her way and never has she said a declarative sentence in her life. It is sad, true, but it is her reality and for sure we are trying to fix it. John and I were together this one day. Actually it was our anniversary, so I know it was November nineteenth. We were able to drop Elizabeth off, have lunch, and then pick her up. Usually I arrived on time, but today we were early and John and I peeked in the window to see the class.

What we saw was Elizabeth up in the front of the class, nervous and near to tears, holding the smile face on a stick, also known as the "conversation smile face." I found out later that the person who holds it is supposed to tell everybody about their day so far and the date, etc. I was heartbroken. She could not talk. She could not say a simple statement. And there she was up there and so upset. I know I wanted her to make gains. That is for sure. And yes, after she had language skills, I would put her up there myself, but not now and not with her near to crying. The staff later said they wanted her to have a turn like all of the other kids, and they knew she would not talk, but that was okay with them.

Well, John and I decided at that point, with the other behaviors she had picked up so far, and now this, she had to leave the school. We decided she needed to really concentrate on speech and then, when she was more verbal, we would look at school. It is so wonderful how God puts you where you need to be at the right time, and we needed to be there that day.

The next day we took her to school would be her last. After I dropped her off, I took the teacher aside to explain our decision. They were understanding but not fully supportive. As I took her home the next day, I told her she was not going back and that we were going to do more, if not everything, to get her to talk. And I said, "You want to talk, don't you, sweetheart?" then she put her little hands on her head, like to hug her own head, dropped her chin to her chest and nodded so very slightly and started to cry. I knew I would remember that moment forever, and then I went home to make some phone calls.

We needed another speech pathologist to add to our list. Kathy would be for whole language, but we needed someone to work the muscles in Elizabeth's mouth so she could get those sounds out. We found a myofunctional speech therapist in another town. Myofunctional speech therapists work with tongue placement, and they help with the forming of words by correcting this problem. In Elizabeth's case, her dyspraxia made moving the muscles in her mouth hard to do. Our purpose with this therapy was to work her mouth and get those muscles to work. Then she could form the words, and we would have beloved language.

This therapist did things like blowing up balloons to strengthen Elizabeth's lips, brushing her mouth with lemon glycerin swabs to stimulate it, and doing tongue exercises to loosen up her mouth before the therapy began. Clicking her tongue and moving it from side to side was also helpful for her. The therapist would have Elizabeth make sounds over and over, and then she would break each word down into syllables and ask Elizabeth to try to say them. We tried to do what she asked, but again, here is where the sensory integration dysfunction would make it so hard. Then we would have tears and fighting and *it was hard!*

Then one day in middle December, Elizabeth said a whole sentence from a Dr. Seuss book. Every word was broken into syllables but she did it, and I was the happiest mom there ever was. I almost cried, but I was too happy to even cry. It was the greatest sound I ever heard. And just in time for Christmas!

I was excited by this turn of events, but there was more during an evaluation by this therapist. She said that Elizabeth was "a dyspraxic, *extremely bright* four-year-old." Yes! She *is* very bright! Now wasn't I telling people this for a long time? I think I was! It was there on paper, everything I kept saying to all the people I had encountered so far. I was thrilled she wrote, "This child is extremely bright and motivated, and she wants desperately to be able to talk." I was so pleased to hear these things, I know it did not change a single thing in our actual day-to-day life, but it was so wonderful to hear it nonetheless.

We were humming right along for a while, as we were seeing the therapist three times a week. Our progress was great to watch, but I could see the therapist was quickly tiring of dealing with Elizabeth and her defensiveness. I think she thought that Elizabeth would greet her warmly and be ready to work, but it never happened that way. Elizabeth was always reticent and scared and cried, and this was every time we went and, again, we went three times a week. We had such a long warm-up time, and the therapist would look irritated as I would try to explain the signs of Elizabeth's shutdown or why she cried a lot or why she did not do what was asked right away. I even had Mary talk to the therapist and give her some calming exercises to do with Elizabeth.

The therapist did try them with Elizabeth, but I know she was waiting for Elizabeth to calm down right after them and get right back to work, but it never happened that way. I could see her tiring of all this extra stuff she had to do to accomplish a treatment. She got irritated and started to take a firmer stance with Elizabeth, and even told me to spank her and let her know that we just were not going to put up with her behavior. She said Elizabeth had to understand that she needed to work!

I am ashamed to say at this point it actually crossed my mind that, "Hey, maybe I should just yell and get things done," but thankfully that thought came and went so fast. I felt bad enough about our situation as it was, but

I felt so much worse after being in the presence of this therapist. She was actually angry with our child.

At one point, during our last session ever, she tried aversion therapy on Elizabeth. She actually flung water on Elizabeth's face when she cried, to get her to feel something unpleasant when she was upsetting someone else. I was stunned into immobility for a few seconds, and then I think I said something and good-bye, and we left. The entire way I cried for this sweet, complex little child. She needed help; she needed caring, and she needed to be safe, not made to be afraid again.

I decided we needed to move on to our next place on our journey, and I truly did not know where that was, but I knew that it was not here. I mean good things happened here, but the therapist has to fit the child and their needs, and it was apparent that she did not fit our needs. Please, to all who read this, follow your instincts and do not look back. I am proud to say that I got my daughter out of an environment that was not a good fit for her. We got such a gift from our endeavors. Elizabeth started to talk, and that was the good that came from all this. She has a little voice, and I heard it, and it was simply wonderful.

I wrote in my journal about Christmas that same year of all the fun things we did together as a family. I wrote:

> It really was so fun this Christmas time. Elizabeth had fun with her sister, playing in the snow and riding on the sled. We had a party at our house, and Elizabeth danced with her Uncle Marc and Uncle C.J.…. we were so blessed to have us all together and share this time. We are so proud of

Elizabeth and all her growth and efforts and her new words and talking.

I love that I was able to say these things. All of our efforts were paying off. The world was starting to open up to her and appear less frightening. I know we have so, so much more to do but, wow, it was great to see the changes!

Let me tell you about Elizabeth's two beautiful uncles. They are my brothers and are officially the two best brothers in the world. John and I love them and adore the attention they dose on our kids. My kids love and adore them. They are a great source of support for John and me and are full of love and fun for our children. There have been so many times when I didn't see the forest for the trees, and one of my brothers would mention something good or new that Elizabeth did, and I would then see it too. And let me tell you, in order for someone to notice subtle changes, they have to have been so involved already. And my brothers were. I would not trade these two men for anything in this world. I have always been close to my brothers, and I love how that fact has never changed; it has just gotten deeper.

I also have to mention Elizabeth's beautiful Aunt Lyn. She is my brother C.J.'s wife and is truly the other half of him. She is fun, energetic, funny, and loving. My kids love her, and they can't wait to hang out with their aunt any time they can. And she loves these children for sure. My children are so lucky to be surrounded by this much love and by these beautiful people. Our children have such a core of support, as do John and I, and we are blessed for sure.

I loved the positive changes I was able to journal about. I felt like, *Okay, we are on the right road. As long as we continue to do the work and invest the time and effort, then we can accomplish anything.* And let me tell you, that was a great feeling. I would look at Elizabeth and see this little girl who was so closed up by fear, who was now smiling and enjoying things that she should be enjoying. She was smiling more and laughing more. I know in my heart she will continue to grow and learn, and I also know in my heart that it will take a lot more work, but when you get such positive results, you know you will continue the efforts.

I think one of the greatest things is that Emily has a sister now. Elizabeth will play in the snow and run with her. She will go to the park with her. Emily loves that she has a sister who will do these things with her and not just cry and scream. I love seeing this relationship between them grow. I have always prayed my children would be as close and loving as me and my brothers, and here it is … the beginning of their friendship. And I love it.

I Am Just So Nervous All the Time

I wish that at this point in Elizabeth's life that I was doing well. I wish I could say I felt calm now and happy, but actually just the opposite was the case; I was starting to feel anxious all the time. Not just when Elizabeth was attracting untoward attention, but always ... in any setting. The library, the grocery store, church ... and forget about sitting in a restaurant. It was like torture to me; I just wanted to get up and leave. I hated being anywhere I could not easily leave. I think over the years I became conditioned to want to hurry. To leave quickly. To be on guard always.

At church, I would never sit in the inner seat of a pew. One time I almost lost it in an elevator once the door shut. And I did not know what to do about it. I know it started with Elizabeth and how anxious she made me in public; but now as things calmed to a degree, I should feel better, not worse, and certainly not in situations where she was holding her own, when I should be proud, not nervous. It was like I had post-traumatic stress over this child. I would have to dig really deep inside me to continue each day. I really would have liked to just stay home and stop the world, not go out into it.

I would like to say that this anxiety just went away, but such was not the case, as I battled it until 2006, with a pit stop on an antianxiety medicine somewhere in the middle. I know my beautiful Elizabeth was worth every bit of everything we have done, but this battle scar that I was left with was and is so hard to deal with sometimes. I would pray that God would help me be calm and peaceful and that He would take this from me. But then I thought maybe this was meant to bring me closer to Him as I battled this. I just know I prayed a great deal before, but now I was in constant prayer, so I was definitely close to Him. It is interesting, but praying on one's knees at one's lowest point is so powerful and meaningful, and something I won't forget.

I will say that my anxiety is something that is with me, and it is a part of me. But in small doses now. It will, I am afraid, always be there in me, as I am the person I am now. I will never go back to the carefree person I was, so I will never lose this anxiety. I sometimes feel just a little bit sorry for myself when I think of how very low I got and how sad I was.

Then I feel sad for Emily, as I know the "feel" of our house was sad at this anxious time. I could see signs of Emily looking stressed. She had trouble sitting down for meals, and she seemed to go from one activity to the next. She seemed a bit lost in her days, kind of like she just did not know who to go to play and be happy with. She needed me to tell her that all was well and I just could not, as each day for me felt forty-eight hours long.

John was my most wonderful support; I could cry to him and tell him anything, and he never judged me. He would hug me and tell me I was allowed to feel anyway I wanted, and I knew he was there for me each day. Together he and I tried to keep our family functioning as best it could at the time. And we did it. We made the best out of the worst, and I love him for all his love and strength.

I will say that I do not recognize the person I am now versus who I was before June 29, 1997. I am so much more assertive and strong and accomplishing. I value all of the little accomplishments my Elizabeth does. I value my kids and the very essence of time with them more than I can say, and I feel my kids all have a great value system due to the gift of our journey with Elizabeth. And that is the good that God promises will come.

My family was a huge support for our family during this time. They would try to understand what was happening in our world and simply love us. My mom would have Emily sleep over and give Emily a break from her world. Emily was officially wined and dined to the nth degree, and boy did she love it and deserve it. It was not an easy time, and I love my husband and family so much for being my strength when I really did not have anything left. To this day, I know my husband and my family will always be there to laugh or cry with us and always love and support us, and it is beautiful.

Something else wonderful happened around the time we left our myofunctional therapy. My older brother, C.J., is a very religious person who told me about a prayer session that his church was having. Actually, it was a guest speaker who was also a healer. I had never been to such an event before, but something told me to be there that night. I remember telling John and my mom that I wanted to go and have them pray over Elizabeth and for her speech. I received the support I needed, and my mom said she would go with me while John stayed home with Emily. I remember saying to my mom that it would be so incredible and beautiful if my Elizabeth would turn to me after the prayers and talk to me. I cried as I told her of my deepest wish. And like always, my mom was there for me and with me.

We took off to the church, and it was so busy. It was about eight o'clock at night, and the speaker talked and talked, and we kept walking Elizabeth around and around and then the speaker said he was leaving. I thought, *Oh, no, now what?* I mean, we had been waiting for three hours, and then we were done? I decided to walk up onto the stage, and I interrupted the speaker to tell him that I needed him and all the people there to pray for my child. And he was so surprised and so willing to do it, even though I later found out his plans did not include healing that night. I knew I had come this far and would not be happy otherwise.

Everyone near to him got on the stage, linked hands, and he told them to pray for this child and for God to give her the gift of language and for her then to use the language to praise God. It was probably the most moving night of my life with Elizabeth. I loved the feeling of love we got and the wonderful feeling that God was right there with us. I left that night really a new person. I was so renewed in my faith and love for God that when I replay this night in my head, I can still feel all the warmth and love.

I was letting Elizabeth drink a Sprite that night and as I left the session, I pulled the blue ring from the bottle and put it on my key ring to touch every day to remind me of that night and God's love. I still have it on my key ring to this day. I know she did not turn to me and talk that night, but we got a wonderful gift. And I know Elizabeth loves God and is a very spiritual child and only God knows if that gift came from that night also.

Music to the Ears

Happy Birthday, number five. Well! A lot occurred since we left the myofuctional speech therapist. We were still going to our sessions with Maureen, as we had been all along. She and Mary would work on similar things, with phone calls to each other to stay on the same page we were, which was great. But here was the best news: we had enrolled Elizabeth in a traditional preschool. We found out that a friend ran a preschool, and that she would keep an extra eye out for Elizabeth and her needs. So she was going to preschool and loving it. She was playing with the kids and doing the activities, and she was happy! She still had her guard up for new things, and at times she would crawl under a table or go behind a chair if she was overwhelmed. And trust me, these preschool teachers had not seen anything like it. But she was there!

So we had to take the time to educate the preschool teachers on sensory processing disorder and dyspraxia.

We had to tell them why Elizabeth may be unwilling to try something and why she would shut down. We also showed them some exercises to do with her to calm her and when to give her some quiet time to herself to calm her anxiety. And they listened, and it worked. We had to educate them on dyspraxia and why new tasks were hard for her to learn, but that with repetition and patience she could do things. And she did learn and try new things.

We were so happy to see her in this setting and above all, she was happy. It's funny, though, I never felt sad to see her go to school. You know how most moms cry when their child goes to school for the first time? I did not do this; I was rejoicing in her success and happiness. I was so happy to see her thrive. Truthfully, I was a touch panicked when I left her the first few times, and I know I called the school repeatedly, but I could not help myself.

This grand birthday number five was celebrated with balloons and cupcakes at the preschool, and she did great. Can you imagine how fantastic that was? She was here in our world now, not in her world of fear, and she was functioning, not locked in dyspraxia. Oh yes, there was always more work to do, but one does need to relish to exhaustion the good, and this was definitely the good.

Also at this point we found another speech therapist who was sweet, kind, and loving. In other words, perfect for us. She was an articulation speech therapist, meaning she corrected the clarity of speech and its sounds. She would go over the sounds with Elizabeth, over and over. We would work on sounds at home and if mastered, we would get to the next sound. We saw her once a week at her house, and we practiced daily.

We were lucky to have heard of her. Again I say our path was guided, as Dawn's name was given to us by a therapist who worked with Maureen. I was talking about our speech needs, and Dawn's name just came up. If you are in need of a new therapist for any reason, it is so important to ask the therapist you know and trust as we did, and maybe they will know of someone or someplace you can call.

I called Dawn and found her to be so nice and calm. And she never once changed that disposition. It was nice to have gains made and to hear Elizabeth saying words more clearly. Dawn had such a kind way about her, and she said she felt so sorry for Elizabeth when she got anxious; but Dawn was able to get Elizabeth to stay on task. She was understanding and curious about sensory processing disorder, and she was willing to learn how to work with Elizabeth. And she showed Elizabeth a great deal of love and for that, we are so very, very thankful.

I will say to those who are looking for speech therapy, please know that a great deal of the cost may be out-of-pocket. We checked with our insurance company and sent them a bill and were rejected. We appealed it and were denied again. And honestly, could you name a better child to receive speech therapy? But we were still rejected and, trust me, I hope they were not recording my phone call on the day I stated our reasons why we needed to appeal our case! I did say that once a child reached a certain age, the insurance company will look to the child's school system to meet their special needs. And some may deny the speech service as ours did. I say this because speech therapy is costly. Once denied, we simply began to pay for it ourselves and continue to do so until this day.

As I said before, we still did all the sensory diet and exercises prescribed by Mary each day. (Sadly, Maureen was starting to fade out of our picture due to her talking about taking a job in a school system.) Mary told us that in this sensory diet, the protocol of brushing and joint compressions were repeated every two hours in order to allow the body to relax and to allow the input of sensory information and learning. Then, when the body was in a place of equilibrium or balance, the brushing protocol may be decreased or stopped all together. In our case, we followed the protocol for over a year.

We did a number of new things from Mary, including blowing through straws into thick liquids and blowing cotton balls across a table with a straw. Picture how much fun that was for Emily to do alongside her sister. I mean, don't we always tell kids *not* to play with their food? Well, not only was I not saying it, I was providing the straws and melted ice cream. I tried to make it fun, even though for Elizabeth it was hard work, and I had to keep encouraging her. But that was how I got the therapies done.

Mary had her drinking with a curvy straw using her lips only, not her tongue and roof of her mouth. We had to work up to twenty-five times each session. Mary also had us using a trapeze bar to hang from, and Elizabeth would lift her legs to work her core muscles. Mary wanted Elizabeth to do a windmill motion with her arms, then arms out to her sides like an airplane.

Mary wanted to get Elizabeth's fine motor muscles exercised by building with tinker toys. And we did sound exercises like saying "Oo" and "A-oo," with exaggerated facial expressions to go with the sound. Mary added another component to the language: I was to play naïve and ask Elizabeth questions about everything and have her attempt to answer them in order to get her to think and talk. She also wanted me to add in the development of concepts such as *more* and *less, empty* versus *full*, etc. Whew!

It did seem like so much but again, it was so all-encompassing of her needs and with each area of need being addressed and worked on, Elizabeth's whole body and thinking processes were growing. Then all areas were adjusted as she grew and changed. It really was a great deal to do, but how could I not do it if it was such a fit to all her needs? Even as I write this, I know it is all about finding out how to make it fit into your day and then doing it each day. And we did.

In addition to those things, we began to address the auditory processing problems that Elizabeth has. When someone has these problems, listening and following directions are hard for them. It challenges the processing of auditory information. It affects their understanding of environmental sounds and voice and speech sounds; their understanding of connected words in language; their understanding of social language structures; and their use of words, or pragmatics, and reading. So sometimes the words we say are heard in a different order, or they may be garbled in their ears. Or they may hear the words, but then be unable to give the appropriate verbal or motor response. Anxiety only serves to make the situation worse. And in my child's case, she was filled with anxiety.

So we had ourselves quite a problem. Elizabeth would have this processing disorder to deal with, along with her other two problems. So for her, if we asked her to do something, anxiety would kick in right away. Then she would not want to touch anything new or attempt anything new. This was the sensory part. And finally, the dyspraxia would make the motor part of the request hard for her. Can you imagine fighting all of these variables each day, all day? I feel sorry for Elizabeth. She really is the hardest working child I know. I will say that asking anything new of her would be very, very difficult and so, so tiring.

I remember so many times when I would make a simple request for her to do something, and I would see her anxiety start. Then I would see her reach for the item, get close to it, pull away, try again, almost touch it and then, once she had it, her muscles would be the next problem to deal with. Then the tears would start, and then the anxiety would escalate from there and sometimes, after repeated urgings, she would just stop all activity and simply look at the table and shut down. It was hard to want to teach something so badly and very seldom being able to do it calmly and peacefully. I wanted her to catch up, so sometimes I would push too hard, and I still do that to this day. I just want her to learn and grow. Each new thing took so long to do, or sometimes even to try to do. So since her auditory processing problem adds to the big picture, Mary wanted to get it addressed.

Mary P. introduced us to a program from a company called Advanced Brain Technologies, and I referred to it before. It is called The Listening Program, or TLP™. This program consists of specially formulated or modulated music, as I mentioned before. The way the program works is that your child listens to it with specific headphones for a specific amount of time. The version we used included eight discs in the set we bought, and then there were other single discs we bought as Mary told us Elizabeth was ready for them. The music in each disc is formulated differently, and each is intended to achieve different effects. The discs accomplish different things within the ears, nervous system, and the brain, and then as a result, you will see changes in mood, anxiety, willingness to try new things, ability to process requests or commands, language, and even in sleep patterns. Sometimes the disc creates that bad-before-good-comes phenomenon, and that can be so hard to take.

But the good does come. We are still using the music program, and I still revel in the changes the music makes in Elizabeth.

Currently, we are now listening to the TLP™ on a specially formatted iPod, with a trade name of iListen, with an even newer headphone with a bone conduction adaptation on it, and the results are even better and faster with this system. Bone conduction, in addition to hearing the music, helps the music get into the ears and body better. These systems are not inexpensive but are so very worth it, and I know it has played a huge part in Elizabeth, not to mention the calm it brings to her system. And that in itself is priceless.

Mary explained the process of using the system. She said initially Elizabeth would listen for fifteen minutes each day, and that I was to note any changes, be they positive or negative. I was excited about trying this system, but first I had to get my little wonder used to the feel of headphones and music in her ears. So we would sit together and I would put some classical music on the headphones, note the time, and try to engage her in an activity like a puzzle or a book. I would try to get her to listen longer and longer each day until we reached the fifteen-minute mark, and then I called Mary and told her we were ready to start the program.

I will say that Elizabeth did surprisingly well with the sensation of the headphones and music. We began the program in the late winter, when she was five, and I was happy with the changes we saw for sure. There were a couple of discs that were a challenge to her system, and she would be angry or growling and hard to get along with. It was tough, and I would call Mary and beg her to help us cope, or change the music, but Mary always talked us through the crisis. She said we should add some calming activities, like jumping and swinging and to brush her more. Mary also told us to keep our demands to a minimum. So I did as told (remember, I am a great listener!), and we were able to get past these unpleasant times.

For those who begin this program, please be aware that it takes time to acclimate the child to the headphones and also make notes all the time for any changes you notice. That way when your therapist in charge of the music asks any questions, you can quickly refer to your notes. You might not believe it, but all of the changes are very important, even if your child does some simple task or makes a simple, new request, the therapists want to know it all. So for sure, this has been a big year for her and a good year, and a happy new year!

If I had to describe our life with Elizabeth at this point, I would say it was so much better. Elizabeth was easier to be with and happier. We took our second vacation that year, and it was more fun for her and Emily than the previous one. Emily was happier, due to having a calmer sister. I did not have to be in Elizabeth's field of vision each minute, so I could trust she was not going to automatically cry if I got that beloved milk for Emily or if I went to change the laundry from the washer to the dryer. She climbed the playground at the park on our vacation, and she was happy to trick or treat. She was trying new things - her way, granted, but at least she was growing. I know I was so happy to think how far she had come. And I know I am thanking God for guiding us on this road that has twisted and curved from the start.

December 1997, in denial.

Emily has always been a great big sister.

Winter 1997, sitting propped up—
she was unable to do it herself.

One year old and eating that hard
bread she loved so much.

A typical morning of crying.

Fear in her eyes and the ever-reaching arms for mom.

Family leaf raking, but she doesn't leave my shadow.

Christmas 2009, crying in typical form, not playing.

June 2000, Elizabeth's third birthday, eight months into our therapy with Mary. Elizabeth is happy and bright eyed.

Christmas 2000-Happy and festive,
it makes our hearts dance.

Loving her hugs from Mimi.

Here is a picture of those bracelets she loved so much.

In 2004, at Elizabeth's kindergarten, she
dressed like Strawberry Shortcake.

Having some snowy fun in 2005 with her sister and dad.

Happy and calm.

My beautiful family, minus my brother C.J., who is
taking the picture. (Michael was taking a nap.)

Dressed for beach day at school.

In 2007, she loved her big bouncy party.
(Elizabeth is in pink.)

Our three blessings.

Elizabeth's school photo in 2010 at 12 years old.
She was worth every bit of effort, just look at that smile!

She's Got to Learn!
She's Got to Hear!

Wow! She is six years old and our journey along with more changes, continues! I bet everyone is wondering, *Did this child get those tubes or not?* Well, the answer is *yes!* She got them just as she turned six years old. I just can't believe the road we had to follow to get them. The ENT we were seeing maintained his hard-lined approach, so I was thinking of getting that second opinion. (I wonder if my reason for not getting that second opinion before now was due to how difficult Elizabeth was to examine and literally how combative she could be. I, myself, must have not been ready to fight that battle, due to how much I was fighting just to hold my head above water each day.)

Prior to starting with Dawn, I had another ear check scheduled, and I asked the doctor if he could write a letter of recommendation to our insurance company so we could get speech coverage for Elizabeth. (Remember the denial I mentioned?) I was sure he saw our need and would see how much Elizabeth would benefit from the therapy, right? Well, he said no. Just no. I could not believe it. He did not offer a reason or even blink as I stared at him. I started to tell him the reasons why he needed to help us, and he said, "You have a developmentally delayed child, and it is time you accepted it."

That was it. That was his reason. I was so stunned that, for a brief moment, I was really unable to do anything. I looked around the small exam room, and I saw the looks on the nurse's face and on the face of his assistant. And I saw pity. Plain and simple. They just felt sorry for me and Elizabeth. I felt so hot and closed in, and I just wanted to leave. He was mean, cold, and heartless. I wanted to do the right thing for my child, and I was being told there would be no help from a man who was in a great position to offer this help. He was not being asked to pay for the therapy, only to write a letter. One that I knew would be typed up and sent out by someone else. So all he really had to do was talk into a tape recorder. *And he would not do it for us.*

I know now he really did not get it at all. Did his comment mean you just give up on your child because she has a delay? If anything, you do more, and you don't ever stop trying. I felt so betrayed, because I trusted him to be on our side and help us. So I told him, "The next time you come home and your son greets you and tells you about his day, I want you to think of Elizabeth." And then I got our things together, and we left.

I resolved not to allow the tears to flow until I was safely in the car, and to this very day, I still cannot believe that comment he made. And that was after three-plus years of being her ENT! What makes it so much harder is now I wonder if the attitude that he showed us that day was his true, but hidden, attitude all along and, therefore, the real reason he never put tubes in her ears. I mean, did he think it was a waste of effort for her and that it would not make that much of a difference? I can't help but think these things, and then I think of the time wasted. Three-and-a-half years wasted! I try not to think about time wasted, because I do believe all things happen for a reason. But in this case, I wonder if Elizabeth would have made gains sooner if he had truly believed in her and done all he could for her.

I guess this is the part where, again, I say to all, if you are not sure if someone is on your team or not, it is time to think about making a change; and then don't look back. I should have picked up some vibes that all was not well when he just would not budge on the tubes and that he was irritated a number of times as he checked her, but I did not. I was so caught up in getting her from point A to point B, that I did not take the time to read his facial expressions or notice his mannerisms. I wish, of course, that I had. I did make a change, but it took the proverbial brick to fall on my head for me to do it.

We are fortunate to live in an area with a great ENT group, located forty-five minutes away. We did not pick them for Elizabeth in the beginning because a colleague of mine knew that the office of the initial ENT was in our city, and they had an audiologist in the office also, thereby eliminating the need for us to go elsewhere for the hearing tests and tympanometry testing.

This new office was a little off-putting to Elizabeth, but they were very patient, and we were able to get her in to see a pediatric ENT. This made all the difference, as the doctor had enormous patience, and she was ready for anything a child could dish out. I explained Elizabeth's needs to her, and she was understanding when she examined her. I will say, though, that her initial remark upon entering the room, carrying the over three-inch-thick chart that was our history of ear problems, was, "What are we waiting for? With all this history, let's just get those tubes in and get her some relief."

I could not believe it! It was that simple. One sentence and we were on our way. No begging, no waiting. We were on the surgery schedule for a little under two weeks, and that my friends, was that! So I was happier than I could believe. I did wish, of course, we had made this move earlier, but we were on our way!

We arrived at the surgery center with a nervous tummy (okay, mine not Elizabeth's). She was actually okay until they called us back and we had to change her and sit with her as she was in the gown and on the gurney and waiting, waiting, waiting, for the time she was taken to the OR. She started to show signs of a breakdown, with a lot of fidgeting, crying, and pulling away from any touch or attempt to hug or hold her. She was almost combative.

I was getting nervous, as per usual, when the nurse said she thought the only way to get Elizabeth through this was to sedate her. I looked at John and said, "We need to talk this through." John said he hoped we did not have to give the sedation, as that meant a risk to Elizabeth from the medication itself, and then a longer stay in the post-op room until the medication was safely out of her system. And then there was the risk she would react badly to the medication and be more combative as it left her system.

At this point I was feeling more nervous, and then I got into my thinking mode, and I thought of all the things I learned about sensory diets. I thought, *I will brush her and do the joint compressions over and over. I will close our curtain, dim the lights, and restrict movement near her and try to allow her nervous system to calm itself and, hopefully, it will work.*

I told the nurse that I needed a little time to try to calm her myself, and she gave a bit of it to me. And I will say it worked; as I brushed, I talked softly. I said soft prayers for God to protect her and guide her through this. I told her I knew she could do this. Over and over I did these things and, slowly, I could see her calm down. She responded so great to the calming sensory activities that I was so proud of both her and me.

John was completely awestruck by what he saw when he returned to our little corner of the world. He was so happy to see her laying on her back with her ankle over her knee and her hands behind her head, just relaxed and waiting. The nurse asked me what I had done because she was getting ready to medicate her. I told her what we did, and she just shook her head like, "Wow!" So off she went, calm as ever.

Isn't it great to hear how well these therapies can help, and that they do work, and that obviously Elizabeth needs them? Thank you, Mary, for your gifts to us. I am happy to report that she came out as calm as she went in, and soon we were on our merry way to lunch and then home. Happy to face the future without ear checks, pain, or loss of speech. We were happy, and she was hearing!

We often went to the pool in our community each summer, and this year was no exception; but this time, we were putting earplugs in Elizabeth's ears before she was in the pool. She could not swim yet, as lessons were not an option, but I found these really great suits that kept her up and floating no matter what. I think even in a tropical storm she would have been on top of the waves, not under them. So she was able to do her summer activities, and swimming calmed her due to its proprioceptive input and the gentle fatigue it induces.

I talk about the pool now because, even though Elizabeth loved it, I clearly know she was watched by a lot of people from our town. She did *behave* differently, and she talked her own way. As a result, *she* was watched and *we* were watched. And it was hard to be there. I hated looking at the faces of the people, who were blessed with typically developing children, as they watched my child. They would talk in their groups. I could see their sideways looks and watch their mouths, and I would be so nervous and, as I said before, it did not take much to get me there anyway, so I would be beside myself by the time we were set to go.

I often wonder why people watch so much. Is it to compare? Is it to gossip? Is it that maybe they wish to know more about what is wrong with the child? Or is it to just have something to talk about that is not their problem, something they can discuss that is so far removed from their lives that it is safe to "tear into"? I know it sounds harsh to hear this, but why else would people talk so much about a child? Why not ask *me* the questions you all are asking each other? I would have addressed them happily, as I would love people to know what my child is all about. But that never happened. Oddly though, I have talked to so many of these same people in conversations many, many times, and yet have they asked what Elizabeth has. No, not once. We have the regular small talk and sometimes more of a conversation, but never am I asked any questions. I am sure "autistic" is the diagnosis they gave to Elizabeth. It is an easy one to give.

I do wish to say to those who do watch others closely, remember they are *people* you are watching who *do* see the looks and *do* feel the uncomfortable attention. And if you are so curious as to watch so closely that you can be noticed, then please make the effort to ask your questions because, in my case, I would have welcomed the opportunity to educate others, and I still do.

To those who are in my position, I can only offer the thought that I know how it feels, I know how hard it is and how much you would give your very being to have things be different. But I say from my experience, be strong, breathe, and pray. And for the moment, be proud of yourself that you are able to do whatever the thing is that you are doing with your child who needs so much. The people watching you have no idea what is involved in even getting your child to the event you are at. Know you did it and more than likely, as it was for me, you did it for your child, not for you.

People always tell me to be proud of all I have done for Elizabeth. I don't generally go about feeling this way but in cases where I feel judged or alone, I allow myself to feel this way and you should too.

As we exit another summer and enter another school year, it became yet again an issue as to where this child would go next. I knew she was six years old (a summer birthday) so she should be in kindergarten for sure, but I didn't want her to go to school in our system yet. I knew her IEP from that preschool had red-flagged her name and that, no matter what, at this point her path would be somewhat set by what information was currently known about her; and right now, the only information was the IEP.

My biggest wish at this point was to work with Elizabeth and her speech team to get the language stronger, and to keep up with Mary and her activities, and push her to make gains in the hope that when Elizabeth went to the school, she was simply more ready. I knew that she needed socialization, and I knew she was now so fond of activities that she needed to *be* somewhere other than home, therapies, or preschool. But where? At the time Elizabeth was six, in our state, your child was not required to go to kindergarten, so I had one more year. I advise checking with your local school system for the laws and requirements that pertain to your state.

I really did not have anything against our system itself, it was just that our initial experience, from the testing through the smile face on a stick, left us feeling bad and on guard. I came to know our situation was being monitored by the school system when I was called by two members of the systems administration. I was asked why we took her out of the special needs preschool (even though it was a while ago), and then I was asked why I thought we had the right idea for Elizabeth needs. I was told that I would be sorry that I followed my own plan for her. And lastly, I was told I should just hand her over to the professionals who knew what they are doing.

I could not believe (yes, so many times I use this expression, but it seems to fit all the time) I was being talked to in this fashion. I, for one, had not talked to anyone in our school system since we left the smile-face-on-a-stick school, and *they* were telling *me* I would be sorry. We had made so many gains since, and taken so many big steps, that I could feel my resolve strengthen. She was still mine for one more year, so I made a statement, indicating that when I was lying in a doorway dead, they would have to step over me and only *then* would they get her.

Yes, it was harsh to say, but I had every reason to say it and to be wary in general. To be told I would be sorry just made me sad. How dare they think they know what my child was about? She had grown a lot. She was so different from the child they knew, and I knew they had no idea of all the work we had been doing. I would never do something that could harm her, and I felt I was being accused of doing just that. I wanted to present a newer and better Elizabeth to them (kind of like the bionic Elizabeth). I needed support, not threats or warning comments and, seriously, why pay such close attention to us? She is just one child out of, what, two hundred forty other kindergarten-aged kids. I felt those eyes again, and it was not in my head.

I thought a place each day would be good for her, and after searching and talking to friends, I came up with the idea of a Montessori school for kindergarten. For those of you not familiar with the thinking of the Montessori school, they believe children learn at their own pace, are driven by their own instincts—all under the watchful eye of a Montessori-trained teacher. The classrooms were set up with some desks, but they had all the toys and educational material placed all around the room. Maps and puzzles of maps in one area, math items in another, and so on. All areas are accessible to the children so they can move about and access the items they want.

I visited them online, then in person with John and my mom, and then Elizabeth went with us for a visit too! It seemed like a very good fit, actually, because the class had a very relaxed feel to it and was nice and quiet. I knew a great deal of noise or activity would really stress Elizabeth's nervous system, so this environment seemed perfect for her. They had some neat rules too! Like wearing slippers only in the school, and all kids needed a cloth napkin in their lunches. They also had a strict drop-off and pick-up routine, where your child's teacher would meet your car each morning as you dropped off your child, and they would unbuckle them from their car seat. They would do the reverse at dismissal. It was a very orderly and a very calm place.

I met with the director, and told her of our situation and of Elizabeth's needs. She said that she was sure Elizabeth would do well, and that she would communicate the information to her teacher. I was so happy for her and so excited to have her settled in a good environment. I guess at this point I allowed myself to think that she would get all she needed at the school, so much so that I put her speech on hold and kind of backed off on the sensory diet. If truth be told, I wanted to treat her like she was a typically developing child. I guess I thought that since we had made so many gains and had been working so hard that she was ready for just school, maybe all that was wrong with her had been put into a semblance of order and we could now move on into the regular world, leaving our very stressful and very busy beginning behind us. After all, at this point we had been working for nearly four years.

Isn't it funny that I allowed myself to indulge my heart's deepest wish and pretend that all was well with my child, and that all I needed now was to send her into this school? I can remember sitting on a bench on the first day and waiting to go in (after this day, the kids were taken out of the car by their teacher), and as I was looking and waiting for the signal to go into the school, I was still thinking, *Please, Elizabeth, hold it together, don't break down now, keep looking okay.* So talk about a paradox of feelings. I said in one breath, "In you go," and in the next, I was mentally willing her to hold tight.

Yet in mind's eye, I saw the school as a new beginning, nice and clean, while behind us was a hazy gray fog of therapies, crying, and a rollercoaster of emotions. And I was so, so ready to get off that ride for sure! It felt so good to send her to school and pick her up, nothing more. Just like the other kids did. No muss, no fuss. And for a bit, I was allowed to live in this world. But then the reality of Elizabeth and her very special needs returned.

It was beginning to show on the faces of the teachers as they buckled her in in the afternoon. I did not want to see those faces, like they had something they wanted to say but did not know how to, or did not want to, in front of Elizabeth. I wanted to pretend not to see them but, of course, I did not pretend. I called them and talked about their concerns, and it was getting to be apparent that Elizabeth was showing some signs of stress. They weren't overly concerned and certainly did not feel she could not be part of the school but were "just concerned," they said.

Keep in mind that they had met her before and I had talked to them about her needs and disorders before we entered her in the school. But something that is so true is that it is easy for an educator to *say* they understand the way Elizabeth works in theory, but the actual *doing* for, teaching, and living with her and these disorders is totally another matter.

Like I said earlier, Elizabeth does not do things wrong, only differently. It is often hard on the educators because her needs and disorders are a *constant* challenge; they will not go away after the first week. Her sensory issues will always make a new idea or task extra hard, whereas with a typically developing child may be apprehensive just the first few days of school. But for Elizabeth, it is like the first day every day. I think that teachers have a wonderful way of comforting kids on those first few days...but to do that each day and all day may just be too taxing.

That is why it is so important to be as honest as you can early on. Tell the director or head teacher just what they can expect. Give them some sample scenarios so they can visualize what you are saying. Then if they say they are okay with what you have said, you can feel you did your best for your child. They are then willing to try for your child because teaching and living with those differences your child has is where the hard work begins. Generally, most people will not have met and/or worked with someone who has these disorders, and that is a very big challenge.

I was told Elizabeth was doing well overall with the rules. She would put on her slippers, and she seemed happy to be there and that was quite nice to see. But according to my talk with the teacher, here is where we started to run into some problems; in accord with Montessori philosophies, once she had received a lesson with one of the materials, she was free to choose that work and do it as often as her internal motivation guided her to use it. The idea of this is to allow the child to gain mastery of a skill through practice and repetition while developing concentration. I was told each day she wanted to play with the jar full of beans, that she wandered away during the morning meetings, and that she would go lay on the floor in the corner at times (a sign of stress).

In accordance with Montessori philosophy, the teachers were trying to give her the space to adjust to this new environment. Their philosophy is to "follow the child" by observing her behavior and providing an environment to stimulate learning. So they did not insist that she come back to the group or direct her to work with something other than the beans. They said not to worry, that some kids do the same things for a long time and then, suddenly, they have a huge burst of learning. They really were the nicest bunch of people.

I was willing to give it a month or two, but then I again started to feel the familiar pang of time being lost and then the panic of time being lost. I can deal with the pangs but when the panic starts, I am not really responsible for what I do next, as I tend to want to fix things like—um—yesterday! So in accordance with my usual mode of operations, I talked to John, and he and I agreed that even though most of the experience at the school was in her favor, the academic part was faltering; so we had a tough decision to make. Do we wait to see if she has that burst of learning, or do we regretfully move her out and try to find a place that fills all the voids?

The director of Montessori was so nice about our decision to take her out, and she completely understood our reasons. It was nice, though, when she said how well Elizabeth was following the lunch rules and rest time rules and that she was a nice, sweet little girl. That felt so good to hear. Then she simply wished us the best in finding a place that fit all our needs for Elizabeth. We left that situation feeling peaceful and calm and then thought, *Okay, now what?*

One of the hardest parts of having a child like Elizabeth was that even through all her gains (physical, emotional, and language), she was still behind in her growth and there was always work to be done to help her catch up as best she could. Then you had to think about all her needs before you could find any place or person to work with her. It was hard, and at times defeating to think that we have a school or therapy that appeared good, only to be forced to make another change.

I say the one thing that kept and still keeps me going is to see how much growth she is making and the positive changes we keep seeing. It is hard to get the world to bend to your child, so when you feel like you do not know what to do next, allow yourself to take a pause to reflect on the good things that your child has accomplished. It really does fortify you for the next round. And above all, pray. I chose to pray in a thankful fashion and just sit and reflect for a moment. Then I went into the mode of figuring out what to do next.

I think if Elizabeth had just one of her disorders and not both, or just had an auditory processing disorder without the ear infections, I know we would have had a much easier time helping her find her way in the world. But we were fighting all these factors, while at the same time having to stand our ground about our beliefs in her abilities. Then add into the mix the pressure we felt from the school. It was tough, and I think I fully realized for the first time in her life, truly deep in my heart, that she would *always* need just that little bit more than the other kids; that in truth I could not fix her, at least not in the truest sense of the word; that she would always learn things her way; that even as she was learning and growing she was *always* going to need some extra time or help to make those gains.

And lastly, I realized that we would need to remain those few steps ahead of each next big decision we had to face. I was glad for this realization because as much as I initially wanted to "fix" her (as evidenced by my thinking prior to her entering Montessori), it was at this point that I saw her as the beautiful little girl she was, who would always have these disorders. That she was a little girl who was achieving and growing, but who we would always have to help. I think that once you fully understand where you are in your situation with your child and what you have, you can really be clear on your plans and goals. I know it made me say okay, we are in this for the long haul, so I will be there for her each day and I will stay ahead of her needs so that I can keep her path in order, maybe then making these future steps easier for her. I was no longer waiting for her to be better or to get better. I was working to make her the best she could be. Each day, every day. We now saw this as the marathon that it was.

One thing that has helped me stay a bit ahead of the current situation is having a therapist to proactively guide me, or a friend with a child who is older to kind of mentor me. It makes all the difference. I had Emily, Mary, and my mom as these wonderful helpers who could see those two steps ahead for me. I saw what Emily did close to three years before Elizabeth was to encounter the same situations, be it teachers, buses, or even clothing choices. I had Mary telling me what to think about next for school, or music or physical development, and giving me suggestions on how to get Elizabeth through the next challenge. And she was always at the ready with resources for me to look up or read. I had my mom, who has a wonderful knack for understanding my children, a sarcastic sense of humor and a love that fueled me through so many, many times when I did not have the answers or a path to follow.

Just do not be afraid to ask for this kind of help. I mean, how was I to know that the certain pair of shoes I picked with Elizabeth were so "Oh, Mom, really?" worthy? (Emily was then kind enough to point out the correct pair for her sister.) Or how was I to think of how to discuss growing up with Elizabeth? Or did I really take into account how Elizabeth felt being the child who was different (my mom here)? Knowing I had help in the wings made it easier and less scary, like that if you might forget to talk about some big point or event, they would catch it for you. I was so busy getting through, say, an average Tuesday that I really was not in the mindset to think about six months from now or if I would pick another pair of inappropriate shoes. I needed and need their help, and I am more grateful than I can say to those who are there to gently turn me in the right direction when they see me stumble.

I say all these things because so many things figure into the raising of a special needs child, things others take for granted; I don't have the same luxury to do the same. I have to think of all things and try to decide what to introduce to her and when, what to put on the back burner for now and when to move it to the front. I think now about the texting phenomenon of the kids today. I watch Emily's fingers fly across the keys like she is typing in the code to save the world from an impending nuclear attack, and I take a pause to think, *Will Elizabeth ever do that? Will she ever want to do that? Is it something she needs to do? Or is she okay without it, and let's put our efforts elsewhere?*

And I do this line of thinking for most things. If she shows an interest, then watch out because I am all over it then; but if not, then I have to decide…push her to try it? Or not? Ugh! It is exhausting. But again, relying on the opinions of those who care, like my above listed people, is the biggest help. So try to line up someone, and it will be a Godsend for sure.

So where was our next stop on our journey? I thought that since the academic part needed to be addressed, could a one-on-one situation be a good thing? I thought that if she had a good stream of positive reinforcements and persons to help her those extra times she needs help, that she would learn well. I thought about homeschooling as an option. But she still needed socialization and, of course, speech and our sensory diet/dyspraxia exercises.

So first off, I called our old preschool and re-registered Elizabeth for the next week. I called Kathy and Dawn and put her back in speech. Then I did something new and talked to the preschool teacher who we liked so well and asked her if she would be interested in becoming Elizabeth's homeschool teacher, and she said yes! We were so excited and so happy to have a plan for Elizabeth that seemed to meet all her needs. She would get some nice socialization at the preschool and then get one-on-one time to learn a kindergarten curriculum. Then get her speech classes in, and all along I would do our assignments from Mary. It sounded great. Busy...but great.

We even turned the spare bedroom of our home into her homeschool classroom. We decorated it just like a regular classroom, and we had stickers, markers, crayons, a desk, and a wipe-off board, and we were excited and all set. The teacher said she wanted to get a copy of the state standards for kindergarten, and she wanted to follow them to make sure she taught Elizabeth well and completely. She was a certified elementary teacher, so she knew what to do.

I remember she started the following week on a Friday, and it went so well. Elizabeth was eager to learn and to be in her new room. I was so excited to see this. God's hand was at work here for sure, as *everything* fell into place for us so fast and so easily that, based on that alone, I was comforted that we were on the right path for us.

Happily, we continued on our way. I loved seeing how well Elizabeth did with her new schedule. She had proved to be quite an adaptable little thing now, hadn't she? Most typically developing kids may not do as well, but she did, and she continued to amaze us at her strength and her willingness to try.

Soon after we arranged all these new things, it was Halloween. Elizabeth was the cutest Spongebob Squarepants® around. I have a picture of her and Emily in their costumes and I just love, love, love how bright and alert her eyes look in this picture. She looked so happy. I wrote in my journal that "she had a party at her preschool and sang the songs there, she trick or treated all of our street, and then helped me pass out the candy. She did *great!* She even helped carve the pumpkin ... what a great day!

There it was, she was in the world and having fun and even touching the pumpkin seeds, etc. . . . whereas before she would have cried at the sensation of the pumpkin insides; I tell you, it really was the little things that kept me going. We made our way through the fall and then into the holiday season and still, all was well. I have to mention here that her language was coming along very well. We were happy to hear her words becoming clearer with her work with Miss D. and our follow-up at home. I had to encourage her to use thinking language and not simply answer with one word, but the words were there.

We had a fun Christmas and over the course of the next two months, she made a new friend in a little girl named Erika. This little girl was one of the sweetest children you would ever want to meet, and she liked Elizabeth right away and, to this day, they are close friends. She had her first play date with Erika, and it was so cute watching her play with a friend and seeing her enjoy this time with a peer. They had a snack together after a bit. So all in all, it was a great start to a wonderful friendship.

These little milestones really meant the world to my heart and soul. It really had been a good year; Elizabeth was learning to read and write better and was enjoying learning. I thank God for all His guidance and gifts. Our Elizabeth was a very different child than she was, and I could not wait to see what else she could do!

I wrote in my journal about our spring family trip to the beach and all the fun we had and we did. We took our trip to Destin, Florida, so it really was quite a drive from Ohio. And it involved a long time in the car, so I was wondering how our girls would do. They actually enjoyed the trip and did so great together. I could see how much Elizabeth was starting to look up to Emily, and how much Emily loved to be there for her sister. Emily loved to show things to Elizabeth and loved to hug her, and especially loved to be her friend. All this was evident on this trip, as we have many pictures of both of our girls, with Emily's arm around her sister's shoulders, and both were close together and smiling.

Emily had so much to offer her little sister and had come to realize that her sister was special and needed more than, say, her friend's siblings. And as much as I wanted to keep Emily from realizing this fact, sort of to protect her from any hurt or pain, it really was for the best that she understood early on. And to Emily it really made no difference; she simply loved her sister, and now Emily was getting back the love and affection she gave so freely to Elizabeth. If I had to think of a reason all this work was done, it would be to see the two of them together and becoming friends.

On this trip Elizabeth was much more relaxed and accommodating than ever. We did not have the best weather, for sure, on this trip. But our little ones made the best of it. We played at the park once or twice, and we even had an afternoon at the mall, where we rode the merry-go-round twelve times. We had fun just being together. And when it did get warm, we enjoyed watching sandcastles get built and stomped on over and over. We played so much and walked the beach, and she enjoyed it all. When we returned, we had only one more full month of school to go. And, like I said, so far, so good.

In May of that year, I had another session with Mary, and we had a very good one. She wanted Elizabeth to hold on to a bar, raise her knees up to her chest, and then land in a pit of balls ten times in a row. I set up all of this in the basement. I got a bar from a playground set and suspended it from a beam with some very strong rope, and then I put plastic balls into a large plastic storage bin and *voilà*: a ball pit. Mary wanted us to get bubble blowers to make Elizabeth pucker and retract her lips, to strengthen her mouth. Mary also had us do a neat button exercise where I put a button on dental floss and then the button would go in Elizabeth's mouth, between her lips and teeth, and I would tug on the string while she tried to hold the button in her mouth, just using her lips.

As for language, I was to read stories and ask Elizabeth what the main parts were and what may happen next in the story, to get some good thinking language going. So we began to do these exercises each day. Mary put us in touch with two websites (www.talktools.com and www. pdppro.com) that were very helpful for those with an oral motor problem or a language delay. They had many tools and toys you could buy to do your therapies at home, such as those bubble blowers. Wrapping up the school year required our homeschool teacher to send to the county office a narrative letter describing what Elizabeth did and what she had learned all year. For our area, the narrative had to come from a certified teacher. If not that, then Elizabeth would have to be tested to show her gains, and then the results of that test would have been sent to the county. We were happy that all was in order and that we were approved for homeschooling for the next year at a first grade level. We were on our way at long last.

I knew at this point that I could relax to a degree. I knew that we had more work to do and, like I said, I saw this for the marathon it was. But I think I should have felt better, for it was now at this exact point in her life that I began to take my antianxiety medication.

I remember that long elevator ride to the ninth floor on this last trip to Destin. I entered the elevator with Elizabeth all wrapped up in a towel, and it was a touch crowded in there. I remember someone looking down at her and saying hi, and just then the doors closed and I wanted to leave this elevator so badly. I did not want people to talk to her; I just wanted out of that moving little box and, *yikes,* the feeling was just awful and I hated it. I remember getting out and kind of shakily walking to our condo, and I was just so tired, so weary. I remember just wanting to stop fighting so hard to keep it together. I wanted to go to a restaurant with my family and not be on edge. Like I said before, just as Elizabeth was most settled was when I began to fall apart the most. I had been battling this anxiety for years, and it was tiring, hard, and sad.

I remember packing up to come home from this trip, and I started to cry to John that I did not want to go home and be alone again in all the places I had to go, and I did not want to keep fighting this by myself. This week together kind of allowed me to dilute my anxiety by knowing John was there to take over if I could not do something. I told John I was so tired of fighting, so tired of holding it together and just so tired of everything being so hard. Part of this anxiety was the wondering what I would do if I could not do something when I had to, and what my kids would think or do if I fell apart near them. I wanted so much to get rid of this feeling that I agreed to try some medicine. And I stayed on it for about a year.

During this year, I was able to feel so much better about everything. I really never wanted to go on anything, but a person can just get so tired of the fight. And I knew I had to be a better and a stronger person for my family, to be able to enjoy them and this life that we had. This road that Elizabeth had us on had definitely left some casualties by the roadside, for sure.

I could count my blessings. I had Emily happy and doing well at school, and happy to have more of a friend in her sister, Elizabeth, who was also doing well. Some of the pressure of being the only one at home during the day to help Elizabeth was coming off me. Her teacher was there to help her, so I was able to hand the baton to her a bit; I was able to go for a run or to the store, so I was less pressured. Yes, for sure, much good had happened.

She Dances, She Hears Again, and She is in Kindergarten

I am happily remembering Elizabeth's seventh birthday. We decided to have Erika over, and Emily had a friend over. So there were four girls here, and we did a craft, we had a candy hunt, and we had a great ice cream cake. Elizabeth did it all, and she loved it. She was so happy. I loved her having a girl party, and it was her first one. I was happy with her behavior all day.

During this summer, I was happy to see Elizabeth use a scooter. It takes a decent amount of coordination to stand on one foot and balance and go forward, but she did it. I thought she looked so happy and proud doing this activity with her sister. These are the types of things she was achieving that were just so "typical" of a child her age but, because it came from her, they were most atypical and fantastic. We did a lot of fun things this summer; we went to the park and to the zoo. She really did a great job just playing and being a kid.

Interestingly, we had an ear check in July of this summer, and we were told that the tubes were coming out of her ears. She did well on the hearing tests, as she wasn't sick or anything at the time of the test. The doctor said that soon the tubes would be completely out and then we would sort of be back to where we were before, watching her for any infections or signs of fluid in her ears. But here was the happy difference, she said to call if there were any problems and "we will get those tubes back in as soon as possible." Yeah, no fighting anymore! So I made a mental note to myself to watch Elizabeth for any changes in her language, such as a decrease in the number of words or a decrease in the clarity of the words.

In the fall of this year, Elizabeth started to watch the movie *Annie,* and she started to pretend to tap dance like Annie did in the movie. So I asked her if she wanted to take tap and baton lessons, and she said yes. So we started her in lessons once a week for the fun of it, and she loved it for sure! Emily wanted to take them also. So my little girls went to dance class and each had a session. Well if you ever wanted to see something cute, it was Elizabeth's little legs with tap shoes on her feet. She did quite well with the early lessons, as there was not much motor planning, but she was having fun and she was doing an activity that was very typical of many kids her age.

The class was only thirty minutes long, so we did not have to really worry about her getting too stressed out; and the activities did involve movement and stretching, so I am sure it was calming to her to a degree. The teacher was so nice and very accommodating to Elizabeth, so this new experience was quite nice. I told the teacher to work slowly with new motor tasks, as Elizabeth would need more tries and more time in order to master the task, and really, all was well and stayed well. And seriously, who would have thought that this little girl would be in a dance class and in tap shoes? This same little girl who, at the age of two and half, would not even wear regular shoes. Pretty neat testimony to the benefits of therapy, isn't it? This tap dancing fun lasted over two years.

So besides tapping and twirling a baton, Elizabeth was being homeschooled for her second year. She was considered a first grader. She learned to read this year. I was so proud of her. And she learned to write, and she learned to do basic math. Isn't that such a sign of how much she was capable of? God bless her! So she was doing the curriculum that all other first graders were doing.

Over the summer, I had spent a great deal of time talking to her teacher and making plans for the next school year. I mentioned to her that we should do some field trips to work on science as well as to the museum and library. So she and I planned our tentative schedule for the fall of 2004. I thought all was well in the relationship between Elizabeth and her teacher, but I started to get a signal that that was not the case. I would start to notice Elizabeth would be very tentative when it was time to go upstairs alone with her teacher. I initially chalked it up to the fact that we just had summer time and now it was work time, and probably all kids were in this mindset. But after two weeks, when it was no better, only worse, I started to be concerned.

I was glad that Elizabeth had other activities on her agenda. I knew she was too old for her old preschool, so in the spring I spent some time reading about the different kindergarten programs in our area (even though she was homeschooled beyond this level). Some were private, and some were affiliated with a preschool. I looked into the latter ones and was so happy to see a program that was in conjunction with a local school system. The system they partnered with had school for their kindergarten kids two days a week, and then this preschool offered the other three days to these same children, thereby making a full week of school. I thought this would fit for both Elizabeth's academic needs and her social needs. She would get to use her year to learn from a state curriculum for kindergarten, see other kids, and learn the rules of a classroom. We met with the teacher, and she loved Miss Elizabeth right away. I was happy and excited.

As it stood, we had Elizabeth in the kindergarten program three days a week, then she had her homeschool time the other two days for three hours or so after attending her old preschool for the morning. On one of the days that she had homeschool time, we would put in a speech class. Then we would be able to do the sensory diet exercises on those days also. I wrote in my journal that I was doing the gross motor and fine motor work.

I thought that with this schedule, all her needs were going to be met, from the social to the academics, from the speech to the sensory diet, and, best of all, I learned how to stay on top of all the situations by asking questions and being watchful. She may have been having some difficulty with her one-on-one time with her homeschool teacher, but she was very happy and very excited when it was time to go to the kindergarten program.

I loved how proud Elizabeth was of herself, going to the school for kindergarten. I loved that Elizabeth had her own school supplies and her own desk, and I loved most of all that she was doing all the things that the other kids were doing. She may not have done them as well and still needed assistance, but she was trying and, for the most part, she was acting like a typical child. She did not get overwhelmed at this kindergarten experience, which was just the best. I was told they had to encourage her more, and maybe give her a bit more help with cutting or coloring, but she was doing it. And all by herself!

One of the cutest things was that she got to wear her new clothes, and she looked adorable. I know it is crazy to say that, but something this small meant so much to me; I got to pick out the outfit, and then Elizabeth would say yes or no to it. I was happy having her be a part of the process, because she never was before (and I got to see her look like a little school girl), and I knew she was happy to be like her big sister and be going to school, too. I felt so excited that she was there and happy.

So, like I said, we were busy, and if I took a step back to look at the big picture, in my mind's eye I saw that our world and each thing we did was like a piece of our life's puzzle. So the speech piece was in order, as was our "Mary work" that I do with her, and her kindergarten and its socialization was going very well, so those pieces were in order also. But the piece of the puzzle that was not looking so good was the homeschooling. As I said, Elizabeth's tentative look made me take pause. I was not sure if we had another problem on our hands, or if it was just a bump in the road.

I knew her teacher was aware of all of Elizabeth's conditions, and they seemed to get along so well the previous year, so I had to admit I was getting very puzzled by Elizabeth's reaction to this teacher. I gave the teacher some ideas on how to motivate Elizabeth to do well in the "classroom."

I would say here that I am a very big sticker chart and reward coupon kind of girl. I loved how they worked and how they positively affected change in my children. The reward coupons were usually homemade and allowed the girls to pick a treat that they really liked. Since they were homemade, they changed as my children changed their likes and dislikes. I have used these coupons to affect some seriously great changes. For example, Emily, at the age of five, used to call for us each night after we put her to bed. I used one of my sticker charts to break this habit. I told the teacher about the charts and stickers, and we talked to Elizabeth about the reward coupon she would get when she did her work and went up to the school room with no tears.

Elizabeth picked an extra movie time for one reward and extra Oreos for the next. (A girl after my own heart on the last one … it brings a tear to my eye.) For the record, television was one of Elizabeth's greatest loves.

She watched it and followed the stories, she laughed at the appropriate times, and she just plain had a ball. But life is not television, so I always limited her viewing and had her do a craft or read or just do the gross motor work, etc. So to give her coupon for her ultimate love should have motivated her so much, right? So I made the coupons, and we gave it a try.

I will say that they did work for a bit, and things seemed to calm down again. But then her teacher started to send her downstairs to me, to have her tell me herself that she was not working. So then I had to take her back up to the room and talk to them both.

This little scenario became very frequent, and it started becoming a real problem for us all. I started to stay up in the room a little bit each time to sort of get the ball rolling in a positive way. But as soon as I left, it would not be much longer until I saw my little Elizabeth's face, and then we would begin our stressful dance. So the coupons were not working. Now here was the thing: Elizabeth was willing to risk upsetting me and her teacher by continually refusing to do her work. She was not motivated by the reward coupons. Something was going on, but what is it? Why was she acting this way? I did not know. I kept a close watch on the situation, but it was hard to deal with all this.

In the midst of all this, Elizabeth started to show some signs that her ears were giving her trouble. Her language started to sound garbled, and the number of words in a sentence started to decrease. She was also pulling on her left ear. So I called the doctor's office and we had a checkup, which showed fluid in her ears. And, drum roll please ... the doctor scheduled us for tubes! That was that. I was very relieved that Elizabeth would feel better soon and, of course, I had the passing thought of how much better this doctor made us feel and how easy she made it for us. I was so thankful, to be sure.

Elizabeth did wonderfully. She received the tubes in January. My mom went with us to the surgery center, and we all even went out to lunch afterward, and she enjoyed a bowl of spaghetti the size of half her body, right after we left the surgical center.

To help Elizabeth understand what was going to happen during this surgical day, I made her a storybook with pictures I drew. I read it to her many, many times in the days leading up to the surgery. It really helped! I knew as the visual learner that she was, it would fit her needs well. It really helped with her anxiety.

I recommend doing this for any event that is coming for your child. There are actually social storybooks that you can find that deal with a number of situations. You just need to do a search on the Internet under "social stories." They are very helpful and are stated in ways that are very clear. They are also tailored to ages and issues and gender. So, good for us, Elizabeth can now hear.

Back to the budding problem with Elizabeth's teacher. I had the thought that maybe she was feeing alone in her education of Elizabeth, you know how teachers can bounce ideas and problems off each other in the teacher's lounge. So I arranged for a teacher friend of mine to come over and talk with her about the classroom set-up and ideas for teaching things, and just anything else she wanted to talk about. So they met and talked, and she seemed happier and calmer, and she did implement some of the new ideas.

But again, all this was short-lived, and our problems returned. It was during one of our conversations that her teacher said something along the lines of "when she stops working, I give a warning then a time-out." I started to get it then that Elizabeth was being punished for her ways again. I bet she was starting to fear her teacher and, because of this, I think she was then on high alert with her anxiety. And once again, when the anxiety was up, her ability to learn was hindered. So then she shut down and it further stressed out the teacher, who then put her in time-out for not listening. And, as you can see, the pattern would continue.

Something Miss Maureen said to me many years ago came back into my head now. She said that kids with sensory issues needed to always end things on a good or high note. Since they remember so much how something made them feel, if there was stress or fear in doing it they held on to that feeling, and the next time the same event or activity came up, they would react badly to it. So with that in mind, I began to question whether we could really erase the feelings now so prevalent in my Elizabeth's mind. Now I wondered if we needed to make another change.

I spent a lot of time talking to the teacher, and Emily spent a lot of time talking to Elizabeth about her feelings and her fears. So with the teacher expressing her complete frustration at the situation, we decided it was time to think of re-entering Elizabeth in our school system. I knew I would do that eventually. The point of our homeschooling was to help her learn and catch up on those things she initially missed out on. I never saw her as being a long-term homeschooled child. I knew she now was a completely different child than she was, and I also knew that when it came to advocating for her, I was a completely different person than I was before. Also, the point was made that Elizabeth loved being with other kids (remember Kathy's initial words from before?), so school was the way.

I made a call to the school and set up a time to meet with the director of special services; John and I agreed to meet with him in a week to discuss testing for Elizabeth, to get her into the school. Due to her previous IEP (that IEP again!), she would need to be tested to determine her strengths and weaknesses and to formulate her education plan based on her needs. And it went quite well. John and I agreed to sign the papers that would give the school the right to test Elizabeth. We found out that the school had thirty days from the day of signing to begin testing (just an FYI).

Our testing had many parts. The school sent their psychologist to our home to administer the actual test on two separate visits; Elizabeth had her speech and O.T. evaluation done by the system, but they did it while she was at her kindergarten program. Interestingly and with a bit of nostalgia, Miss Maureen was the O.T. who did the testing. It was so great to see her, and for her to see Elizabeth. Yes, she was so excited about how Elizabeth had grown and how she was acting. She said Elizabeth was doing so great and she was so excited to see her now since she was the first one to ever work with her. It made me feel good to hear her say such nice things about Elizabeth.

When the testing was done in very early spring, we were sitting around the table, staring at the IEP team. It included the director of special education, the school's O.T., the speech teacher, the special ed teacher and the mainstreamed teacher, those who did the testing, and the principal. It was quite a scary time.

It can be quite intimidating and nerve wracking to be at that table, waiting for results about your child. But if there is one thing I have learned from all my years, it is that you know what's best for your child. Do not be afraid to speak up and be confident in yourself and what you want. Everyone there is really supposed to be there for the good of the child, not to scare the parents. It is hard to speak up when you are talking to veteran educators, but truly do your best to breathe and talk.

They each read their part of the testing and its results. Some were encouraging, some not so much. We heard a great deal of, "She did not appear to test well," or, "It appeared with a little more guidance, she would have been able to accomplish more, but we were unable to do that in the testing situation."

I knew she would not test well; it did not come as a surprise to me. I told them I wanted them to get to meet her and to see her abilities first and then they could add to or change the goals, etc. So I said I would meet with them in late September to adjust the IEP. We signed the current IEP with the above addendum on it, and we were set.

All in all, it was determined that she would be in a mainstreamed setting for homeroom, music, gym, art, lunch, and recess, but in the special education room for math, language arts, science, and social studies. She would have an aide, whom she would share with three other students to facilitate her learning and be there if she needed extra help in any of the classrooms. I felt good knowing an adult would be with her throughout the day.

To those who are in a similar situation with an IEP, it is important to know that the IEP needs to work for your child; it is there to speak for your child to all those who pick it up and read it. There is a part in it that is the narrative of your child. That part covers the typical things like age, sex, etc., but it should also include all the issues or illnesses or problems your child has. And it should read the way you want it to because, as Mary put it, if a substitute teacher picks it up to read it and it does not explain why your child may act in a certain way or why they struggle with a task, then this new person will treat your child and his or her ways differently than they would have if they knew the whole story. So I really advise you to read it well. Really look at the goals and really think about your wishes and goals for the year. It is hard but very, very necessary.

And one more thing: have your other therapists read it too and offer their thoughts on the IEP and its components. Mary has been of immeasurable help in this IEP situation many, many times. She finds areas of concern, and we address them. You need this help to do it right. Each area of need has its own part of the IEP, so each of our therapists would help in their specialty area. Trust me, use all of the people who care about your child. The IEP is a fluid document and can be changed. When you have a concern or a problem, you are allowed to call a team meeting to address them. You do not have to wait the full school year. I did not know that fact at this time, so please know this is your option. Do not be afraid to call a meeting if you have any concerns and, please, get all requests documented on the IEP, as it is a legal document. If the teachers agree to try something or change something, make sure it is on the IEP form and signed.

I feel that we did our best for Elizabeth in those years when we decided to go against the mainstream and work with her our way. We know she received the therapies she needed. We know she learned and grew. When we presented her to the school, she really was a different child than she was before. I know in my heart we did what was right for her, that we made a huge difference in her life, and I am proud of what we accomplished. The die was cast, and she was officially a student in one of our elementary buildings.

So Elizabeth's teacher and I agreed to continue the homeschooling until school started. This, however, did not prove to be an attainable goal. Emily spent a great deal of time with Elizabeth, so she was able to reach her more than I could; and it was through her efforts that the truth about Elizabeth's feeling for her teacher came out. Emily told me that Elizabeth was afraid of her, and that Elizabeth said "her voice is mean." I felt terrible hearing this. I really felt bad and so sorry for my child. Elizabeth would not knowingly set out to upset someone. She was just being Elizabeth. She needed to be unafraid. And, sadly, she was now afraid in her own home.

It was one day in late summer that, I guess I need to say here, I finally realized that this teacher just could not work with her anymore. I had already trimmed her teaching areas from all academic areas to those of music and art. I figured that it was summer after all, and those two areas were relatively stress-free, so I thought we would be okay.

As a sidebar here, I really do not know why I was even doing school at all in the summer, other than to say we all make our mistakes and that was one of mine. Anyway, I had left Elizabeth and her teacher to do their music time together, with Emily there also (she asked to stay); I had to be gone for fifteen minutes to the post office, and I would be back so fast. But when I got home, Emily had the strangest look on her face, and the teacher looked upset. Later I was informed by my beautiful, brave Emily that, even with her there, the teacher was so tough on Elizabeth. Emily said her tone and actions were sharp and angry, and that Elizabeth cried.

I thanked Emily for her words and her love for her sister, and then I called the teacher and I asked her what had happened. She admitted to being frustrated by Elizabeth's reactions to her, and we finished our talk with both of us agreeing that that would be the last time she worked with Elizabeth. Again, the teacher did help our daughter, but in the end we should have addressed the problem so much sooner.

I question why I waited so long. I wondered if I just so much wanted it to work. Did I wait so long that my child was hurt? I don't think so. Thank God, but I will say I learned from this mistake. If anything does not look or feel right, I address it fully, right away. No more waiting. No more putting Elizabeth at risk. And here is one more big point I need to make: even if you do not want to face making a change, a change that will make your road more difficult, you still need to listen to your heart and do what is right for your child.

Our homeschool teacher had already handed in the year's report for first grade to the county, so we were waiting for the start of school ... in our public system.

That was such a big part of our year, as you can guess, but other things also went on for Elizabeth that were more to the positive. I alluded to the fact that children like Elizabeth remembered the feelings associated with an event or activity. Those feelings are hard to erase and, like Miss Maureen said, it is so important to end all things as positively as you can so they will be more willing to try things again the next time.

We all do this to a degree. But for those of us without these disorders, it is easier to forget the bad and try again. But someone like Elizabeth would almost obsess over an activity she would have to do, if it made her feel bad the last time she did it. I tried to remember this fact when we tried a new game or toy or activity, but one can only bend the world so much to make this happen. So because of that very fact, there are a lot of feelings she has that she would feel so much better without.

Well, years ago, Mary told us about a therapy called craniosacral therapy. It helps with residual anxiety left in the body or tissues after a stressful event. It also relieves some of the tension you feel about an event, or rather the associations you have related to an event. For example, if you were frightened as a child about the circus, then your association of all circuses from that point on may be bad ones. This therapy was designed to help with those feelings and for children like Elizabeth, who have plenty of those associations and resulting stresses.

When Mary first brought craniosacral therapy, or CST, up to me, it sounded so foreign, and I sort of tucked it into the back of my brain. Mary was telling me all the good that this therapy could bring. It helped children release tension and to relax the tissues that hold on to the bad feelings or stress. The name craniosacral therapy was coined by the osteopathic physician Dr. John Upledger, founder of the Upledger Institute, to describe a series of light-touch manual techniques that he had developed to treat a variety of health issues. The following is some basic information about CST that I received from the institute itself:

> CST is a light-touch approach that can create dramatic improvements in your life. It releases tensions deep in the body to relieve pain and dysfunction and and improve whole-body health and performance. And few body structures have more influence over your health than your central nervous system. And few body systems have more impact on your central nervous system than the cranialsacral system—the soft tissues and fluid that protect the brain and spinal cord. Every day you endure stresses and strains and your body absorbs them. But your body can only handle so much tension before the tissues begin to tighten and potentially affect the brain and spinal cord.
>
> Unfortunately, this can compromise the function of the central nervous system- and the performance of nearly every other system in your body. CST releases those tensions to allow the entire body to relax and self-correct. Using a gentle touch—starting with about the weight of a nickel—practitioners evaluate your internal environment. Then they use distinctive light-touch techniques to release any restrictions they find.
>
> By freeing the central nervous system to perform at its best, craniosacral therapy naturally eliminates pain and stress, strengthens your resistance to disease, and enhances your health and

well-being. And because it's so gentle, CST can be effective for all ages, from newborns to elders.

Please visit their website for much more information at www.upledger.com. We decided to try it. I still say that when things feel right, then it is the time to try them. Mary had been talking to me about this treatment for some time, but I never really considered it past the time I left Mary's house. I seemed to be so wrapped up in the more immediate needs of each day. But then, one time I remember thinking that I was ready to take on this one more thing. Mary's husband, Paddy, is a licensed massage therapist or LMT, with a specialty in craniosacral therapy. He provides this treatment that I call "cranial work." But it is really called craniosacral therapy.

I can remember that day that we trekked up to Mary's house, not to see Mary but to see Paddy. I knew this therapy would help Elizabeth let go of some of the stress and anxiety that she held onto. I had so hoped it would make her feel calm. It was at this time of her life that Elizabeth seemed so busy and so active. Sitting still for her seemed so hard. She needed to fidget or fiddle with something always. I wanted something that would make her calm. I knew that my expectations of this therapy were unrealistic. I guess I hoped that one hour of this therapy would do it. How silly that was of me, and you would think I would know better already; but I thought it just the same.

We arrived at Mary's house, and Paddy greeted us. We went downstairs to what we had already come to know as the therapy room. Paddy explained to Elizabeth what we were going to do. Paddy sat on the one exercise mat, and Elizabeth sat near him. He put his one hand over her stomach and one under her back. He kept them there for a while as he asked Elizabeth some questions. I was there for each therapy. As he asked her questions, I could see she was feeling something, as she began to try to move away from his hand, but not in a scared manner. She was not afraid in the least. She was just feeling something from the therapy. Then she was asked more questions, and she started to cry. I wondered what feelings he was bringing out of her; Paddy, of course, was very happy to have her respond to this therapy. Time went so fast and before I knew, it the session was over and it was time to go. Paddy said that he would schedule us for the next time, and he wanted us to know that for a first session she did so well. I guess I was waiting for her to jump and hug me. But instead, we went to lunch and then home.

We continued to see Paddy every other week. And he was great. Always patient and always calm. I could see how Elizabeth looked after these treatments, and I could see she looked like a person who had just been awakened from a nap, and she looked peaceful, like her whole body was relaxed. I learned that this was as most things are ... a process.

Each time we went she would fidget, she would repeat a certain sentence, whatever she picked, like asking if Paddy was happy. Then she would settle down and get to work. She would eventually cry each time. It was like she was getting rid of all the pain she had had in her life, all the fearful times, all the times she could not do what she wanted. I knew this sweet child had had so much to deal with. She was smart, and she remembered all things. So the love we had given her was in there, the good things were there. But so were the hurts and the sadness. She now had a chance to get rid of these feelings, and I was happy to give this chance to her.

I actually had a chance to experience it prior to Elizabeth. Paddy said he liked the moms or dads to have a session, so that we would know what our child would be feeling and going through. I think that was where I became a believer in the therapy. I went to one a couple of days before Elizabeth did. I was lying on the table, kind of thinking, *Why am I here? This stuff can't possibly work.* But something was telling me this was the right road for Elizabeth, so I needed to see what it was all about, for her sake.

So as I was lying there, Paddy put his hand over my stomach and one under my back and kept them there for a long time. Then he asked me some questions, and I was so surprised at what he was sensing. I never told him anything about me or my feelings, about Elizabeth, or even my ache of the week (which was my left hip at the time). I remember him specifically asking me not to tell him anything this day, just to relax and feel how the therapy worked.

Anyway, he proceeded to ask me if I felt guilty about Elizabeth, and I was so surprised that he would know through this therapy what thoughts and feelings I was holding in my mind and in my body. I said yes, I did. I wondered if my silly worries about weight or my worries about my earlier illness had some effect on her before she was born, or even on the issues she currently had. I started to get a little teary over this topic. I was so surprised that he could possibly get this information from just this initial work with me. He continued to ask questions of me, and so many were so dead-on accurate to my concerns, some I really had never said to anyone except John, that I was so, so impressed. And then he moved down to my left hip area and said, "How long has this hip been hurting?" I was awestruck at this point. He explained that we held on to our stresses in our joints and, in this case, my hip pain may have been the result of all my feelings I was holding in. I then became such a believer that this therapy was real and if he could reach these feelings in me—and trust me, I had a lot more than I addressed this day—then I was sure we could begin to help Elizabeth with all she was feeling and had been through.

We went to Paddy a number of times in the late winter and early spring of that year. It was an hour trip to his house and one hour or more of therapy, then the trip back home, so really it was most of our day spent to get this treatment accomplished. We kept up with the treatment until summer, when it really wasn't feasible to drive this much with Emily home for the summer. I really hated to make Emily spend her days in the car and I, of course, wanted summer to be summer. So I needed to find a local person to continue these treatments. I had already talked to Paddy about it, and he supported our decision completely.

So in the early, summer through my mom, we found a special, wonderful, spiritual woman named Miss Jill. She could provide the same therapy a mere ten minutes from our home, and we were on. Now Elizabeth could continue her therapy, and we could continue to see the good come of it. Elizabeth became calmer, and she was very happy to go to the therapies, which told a huge tale. We have been with Jill ever since.

So this year had sure been full of changes, both in the kinds of things we were doing for Elizabeth and in the addition of new therapies. But the thing here was that even through all of this, Elizabeth was growing and talking and doing things. It was like we were gently leaving the world of such a heavy sensory diet and its needs to a world with only a bit of it in it, but the majority was just the world.

Through all the years, we have been working so hard, running to therapies, charting progress, making phone calls, changing therapists … it had been going on now for five full years. But when I take a pause to see this child, I mentally see that Elizabeth had left her world of fear and isolation caused by her lack of speech, and she had entered our world. It's as if she had closed some of the doors to her world behind her, and I feel like she never will go back through those same doors, like we now have her on a permanent level.

I was always so worried that something we did or did not do might scare her enough to cause her to regress. I feared waking one day to see the child she was at two greeting me when the child I put to bed was five or six or seven. I can now say I know she is here. I love her little personality. And I love how she can just smile and win over the hearts of whomever she is with. It is a pretty great feeling for me. Very much a sense of relief, and I'm very, very thankful to God for all the good that has come of such a journey thus far.

I have told you about the changes for Elizabeth related to school, but in the time line that is our history, a wonderful, new teacher agreed to be Elizabeth's tutor, starting in April of this same school year. About the time I reduced Elizabeth's first homeschool teachers to music and art, this new person came into our lives. She is related to Miss Dawn, our articulation speech therapist. Miss Dawn recommended her to us after I had shared our current problems with her. That recommendation was one of the best ones I had ever received.

I remember the first phone call I made to Miss Rosemarie. I was so nervous calling her, because I wondered what I would do if she declined the offer; but she did not. It turns out she is a certified teacher who is a licensed intervention specialist (mild to moderate), and who is highly qualified in all subject areas, meaning she has a license that is appropriate to the grade and subject areas she is teaching (www.education.ohio.gov). The term intervention specialist is, at the time of this writing, used in place of the term "special education teacher."

She works in one of the local school systems as a teacher for special needs children. She sounded so calm and nice. She met with Elizabeth soon after, and I had to go into the school room with them because, as I said before, Elizabeth would not go there without me. Yes, it was that ingrained in her brain and the association of the school room caused such a fear that she would not go, even with a new person. Miss Rosemarie sat on the ground with her and tried to get her to talk, but she was too scared and she just kind of played with her fingers, looking down. I guess at this time I really understood how bad this little one had been feeling in this situation. Like I said before and will again, act on what you feel or sense. At this point, I vowed never again to allow someone to affect her in this way.

Our "classroom" was set up with posters on the wall. Some were of schedules and plans made by the last teacher, and one was used for reward stickers. Well, I saw the look on Miss Rosemarie's face as she looked around the room and her eyes landed on the posters.

She lowered her head to meet Elizabeth's and said, "Do you like these posters?" and Elizabeth shook her head no. She asked, "Do you want to tear them down?" and Elizabeth kind of smiled and nodded. So Miss Rosemarie got up, tore one off the wall and said, "Do you want me to rip it up?" and again Elizabeth smiled and nodded. So she did. Then she said, "What about those other ones? Did you like those?" and then she and Elizabeth proceeded to rip to bits all the charts, plans, and reward charts. Then Miss Rosemarie said something along the line of, "Now we are starting fresh."

Well, that was it; Elizabeth was sold. And this wonderful teacher has been helping and tutoring and loving our Elizabeth ever since that point. Except she has changed; she is not only Elizabeth's tutor and friend; she is like a member of our family. Emily loves talking to her and hanging out with her when she babysits for us. Simply, we love her. And she is one of my dearest, dearest friends. Oh, and by the way, that little conspiratorial glint she had in her eye when she was tearing down the charts shows up again and again, as she has one of the best zeals for life I have ever come across. She loves her sunrises and her sunsets, and she never sweats the small stuff. She was everything we needed all rolled up in one person. Thank you, Miss Dawn, for telling me about your "awesome aunt Ro."

So now you know all about this big year number seven. We had a teacher, she lost her way with Elizabeth, we lost a teacher. We gained a dear friend and teacher combined. We started cranialsacral therapy with one therapist, and then settled nicely on one closer to us. We continued our speech with Miss Dawn and Kathy. We were still doing Mary's work, which was about the same as when Elizabeth was six, with a heavy concentration on watching and recording the effects of the TLP and CST on behavior and language. And above all, Elizabeth was going to school. Wow, what a year! But if you think the surprises and twists are over, I would have to say just wait a bit to hear this next story.

Time to Walk the Walk

Happy Birthday to you, dear Elizabeth. You are eight. Time seems to have gone by so fast for you. I can't really believe you are this old. I guess when you spend so much time trying to catch up to these goals that you have, you don't really realize how fast the years are going by.

I think in my case, I would always compare the age Elizabeth is and all the things she *is* doing to all the things I *want* her to be doing, and then I would focus on achieving these self-imposed goals. I journal a lot about the happy child she is and about how much I love seeing her do this or that. I have a hard time explaining the joy I felt and still feel over any achievement she makes. In my journal, I write about all holidays and events, and I write down something she does that is new and, even as I reread them, I still feel that sense of excitement and that feeling of *Yes, one more thing off the list.* One more thing she will have ingrained in her mind and body. Then we can build on it to achieve the next thing.

I have always been a thinker, and I have always been the kind of person who does not do well with time passing and the end of any event. As a kid, I was the extra sad one when our Florida vacations were over. I would be so quiet in the car on the long drive home. My brothers would be doing their schoolwork and would seem just dandy about going back to school and home. I would be the one excited that we still had two more days to drive, as anything that extended our trip was worth it to me. I would be so sorry to see Christmas be over and I, to this day, absolutely hate the last day of summer, when my children have to go back to school. I miss them like crazy then. I really do not like marking the passing of time, and those markers for me include birthdays.

So here I was, seeing this beautiful eight-year-old, and I found myself praying that I hoped I enjoyed her as much as I could have as she was growing. I think that I did. It was so hard to say if I enjoyed her, or if I was always evaluating the day's events and comparing them to my list of what I had hoped she would she would do that day or in that particular situation. I know our life together has been so busy and such work. I know I was so happy when she was happy or I was so excited when she achieved a goal or learned a new task. But did I enjoy her? I really cannot answer that question. I only hope I did.

As my role in Elizabeth's life was changing from my being her therapist and then being her mom (first and foremost), I had now become, in her eyes, the person who pushed her, who absolutely demanded she tried things. With my deepest heart I believed in her, so I would accept nothing less than her best effort. Well, she and I had come to the time in her life where our relationship had its bumps and curves. And moods. (Mostly hers, but sometimes mine.)

I need to tell all how much I am thankful for the calming, loving force that is her daddy and my John. He is Elizabeth's safe haven when I am upset. He is my support and rock when I am not sure I can face another day. He has been so important to our dynamic, and so strong for our family. John, as I mentioned, has very long hours in a very busy practice, but he would come home and always smile and hug his girls, and even if his heart was breaking over Elizabeth, he really never let me know until she was ten, as I think he knew I really could not take hearing that. Thank you, John, for being you and for being our very foundation. We could not have made it without you.

This was my thinking at this particular birthday, and I knew it came from the fact that Elizabeth was registered for school and, in a way, I was losing her. I was so proud of her, but I was losing her and losing control of her education and of her day.

Don't get me wrong, I rejoiced that she was going to school and she would get to ride the bus one day, just like I promised her when she was four. I remember the day she watched Emily get on the bus. I told her, then my nonverbal child, "One day, honey, you will get to ride the bus and go to school. I promise you. I will work so hard to make sure that happens for you." I still couldn't help but feel I was losing her, and I was scared that maybe they wouldn't watch her like I would, or maybe she would be afraid of something and not be able to tell anyone.

I think, above all, that maybe I was mourning the loss of all the things a mom gets when they have a typical developing child. I think I missed out on the cozy mornings, the hugs under blankets you get when you don't have anywhere to go; the laughter and chatting that comes with any new experience; playing dress-up, watching your child smile and be happy over something silly; or simply relaxing and loving up your child. I did not get those things. And now I officially was not going to get them, because my time with my child at home was done. And, in a way, I felt very cheated.

I don't know if other parents of special needs children feel this way. But it was the way I felt. I saw how much she had gained and grown, and I had heard her great laugh and seen her great smile, and I loved her personality. I can't help but say, "I wonder what life would be like if I could have her be all these things, but at the age of three, and then I could grab those hugs she never wanted to give, or I could take her to lunch just the two of us and know she would not be afraid."

I guess I was mourning the loss of a childhood's worth of fun I did not get to share with my Elizabeth. Yes, this was a rather late mourning phase, as she was eight, after all, and one would think this all would have really dawned on me a whole lot sooner than now. But it didn't.

I know the trigger to this emotional outpouring was thinking of her entering the school system, one that would have her for the next twelve years. Our time together was officially over.

I know Elizabeth had a great summer this eighth year of her life. She took swimming lessons; she was in the library reading club; and she was getting tutored by Miss Rosemarie. I know she was really feeling no fear now in her world, or in any of the activities we were doing. She even got her First Communion in July. Here is how that went.

Traditionally, in the Catholic Church, the First Communion candidates have many special classes or activities to attend prior to the actual First Communion Mass. Then the mass itself was a *huge* event. There were the dresses, and the rehearsals, and the songs, followed by the party afterward. But with Elizabeth, she and I studied the same book the other children did, just broken down for her.

I talked to Jim Merhaut, the director of catechesis, who directed the religious studies of the church. He is a great, patient man. He said that any Mass that we wanted could be her First Communion Mass. He would tell the priest of our situation, and all we had to do was to tell the church office what day she received the communion.

They would then use that date on her First Communion certificate.

So we picked a Sunday, put a pretty dress on her, and she knew what we were doing. And she was happy and so appropriate. It really was like a little angel was getting her First Communion. She looked beautiful, and I cried as her little hands reached up for the Host. It really could not have been more perfect. Our family, together, sharing this special blessing with our child. Emily was proud of her sister. I loved knowing it was done our way. We took Elizabeth to her favorite restaurant for lunch afterward, and that went great too! Truly, a beautiful day from start to end. For those of you in any situation where you need help or that looks too overwhelming, never fear asking for some of the rules to be adapted to your needs. The worst answer you can get is no, and the best answer will be one that gives your child a day or experience they deserve.

I could never imagine trying to get Elizabeth to sit through all the classes and rehearsals. She would have become anxious and would never have enjoyed her day at all. And isn't a happy day what you are trying to give to the child? Later, Emily told me part of her wished she could have had her communion this way, instead of the way hers was with forty other children and all the build-up it had. That said a lot to me.

After this wonderful day, we continued on with our summer. Elizabeth even had her first sleepover at my mom and dad's house. How was that for a real growth? She and I packed her bag, and off she went. After she arrived home the next day, I heard how much fun they had and how great she did and slept. Yeah! What an accomplishment. She was so proud of herself. I think that one of the main reasons she was so able to go somewhere and act so appropriately was due to my efforts with behavioral modification.

As I mentioned before, I had always used my "coupons" to reward certain behaviors, or the standard time-out areas for the untoward behaviors. So I guess I did dabble in the area of behavioral modification for years. But Mary helped me fine-tune it for Elizabeth.

Since our start, our Mary work has gone from the big muscle groups, balance, and stretching, etc., to more precise motor groups, for using scissors or self-care activities, to more thinking activities like, "How did the person in the story feel when…" or "What did we get at the store yesterday?" I liked being able to bring out some of what was inside the mind of this little girl. We needed Elizabeth to use this thinking and reasoning to achieve.

One of the hardest things was changing how Elizabeth acted in public. Thank God, she was this happy child now. She was always laughing and having fun at home, so she wanted that to continue everywhere she went. She was happy to move and dance, and she wanted to move as much as she wanted in public. But she also was uncomfortable answering someone when they would direct a question to her. I know she did this due to her speech delay. She knew she sounded different than other people did and, in addition, she hated to be put on the spot for anything, even something as simple as a common question. It would make her anxious, and she would kind of hide her face or mumble something. It was so hard, because I knew she knew how to answer and that, in most cases, she knew the answer. But out would come something that was not anywhere near to the answer. Yuck! I would cringe inside as I heard it, and I so much wanted her showing the world all she was capable of, not just acting and talking any way she wanted. I expected Emily to be a lady and I expected the same of Elizabeth, so we needed some help.

I guess until now, Elizabeth was not really ready to achieve these goals easily. Like I said before, I feel all things happened at the time they were supposed to. So in one of our sessions with Mary this year, she gave me some great ideas to modify Elizabeth's actions and her thinking, to help her be in charge of herself, instead of me having to tell her each minute of each time we were out in public. I was so excited to try them and actually so excited that she was at this level too. Prior to Mary's ideas, I would use my words to tell Elizabeth how I expected her to act *before* we entered a public place. That did not always work out so well. She would remember the rules for a bit, but then she would start moving foot to foot or spinning around, sometimes laughing or simply saying she was ready to go and not listening to me. Yes, that was such fun. On one hand, yes, it was great that she was a fun-loving, happy girl but, on the other hand, she was not a one-woman show.

So Mary said we needed to make Elizabeth responsible for her actions in public, and have her use some thinking and reasoning to decide how she should act. She suggested making a behavior notebook, and on each page list the behaviors you would like to see for a specific place, like one for the library visit, one for the grocery store, and so on. I listed things like "Stay by the cart" for the grocery store and "Hand your card to the librarian" for one of the behaviors on the library list.

I completed the notebook, and Mary said to sit down and read it to Elizabeth, then read it again each day for several days. Then before going into one of the places, I was to give the notebook to Elizabeth to read to refresh her mind, and then I was to make it clear to her that she was expected to do these things or there would be a punishment. So after we left a place, I would ask her some questions to make her use her thinking language like, "So how do you think you did waiting in the line?" Then I would ask her more questions based on her answer to the first one, and so on, to encourage thinking and to reinforce the desired behavior. Sometimes I would be so happy with her behavior that I would simple tell her that, and sometimes she just did not do well and then I had a lot to ask and talk about.

I will say this activity did lay the groundwork for Elizabeth to realize she was in charge of her behavior and how well she presented herself to the world. She was learning to control her actions and words, and we would be using this as a stepping stone to further modifications. As for the punishments, I sat down with her and told her that I would have her write ten times on a piece of paper whatever it was she did that was inappropriate. For a really big infraction, I told her she would be in her room until the end of the day. And yes, the latter punishment did happen on many an occasion. And yes, it was hard to see and to enforce, but you know what? It also let Elizabeth know we were serious about her behavior and her being inappropriate.

These changes required a great deal of consistency and, for those who are in the same position, it helps to have an idea of the behaviors you want to see, and to discuss with your child ahead of time what you expect of them. Mary also suggested at this time that I write some key phrases on index cards to help Elizabeth maintain control when it looked like she was going to act inappropriately. I got colored index cards and wrote "Stay seated" or "Quiet voices" or "Hands still," or whatever I wanted her to remember. I put these cards in my purse and, when I needed to, I handed them to her to read, and they acted as reminders, and they worked!

The best thing about the cards was that they allowed me to remain silent while they did the work. I will say that Elizabeth has such a fun personality and is so smart that, on occasion, the same card I placed near her was delivered back to me, wrinkled up, and she was smiling with that little twinkle in her eye, telling me that she knows what to do, but she does not feel like "hearing" me again. Yes, she is full of spunk and life. And yes, I made up another card whenever she destroyed one. I was always and will always be a firm believer that behavior can be changed, and I am very willing to work to get my end result. So I was, of course, very willing to try these ideas.

The positive results I got only fueled me to want to do more. I was at a point in our time together that I needed her to be a big girl now. I needed to be able to go places and see a young lady behaving properly. I mean it was different before, when she was afraid of so many places or so many sensations. But now that so much of that had abated, I needed to live with her in the true world, a world that included trips to our mega-grocery store, or shopping for clothes or even shoes. She needed to learn that the crying she was doing before was indeed justified, but now there were other ways to communicate, and certainly other ways to behave.

I am happy to say she rose to the occasion and even asked me at the end of the day, "Are you proud of me?" She knew she did well, and she was quick to learn that indeed she was proud of herself; and *that* was what we were aiming for the whole time. We really were making some great gains here.

It was now fall, and Elizabeth loved her day at school; she loved being with other children, and, I was told, was doing so well following the rules and doing her work. She came home happy and did her homework and had her tutoring with Miss Rosemarie. I was proud for sure of her.

I will say that after all we had been through, I think we had finally found the people who would be our "Team Elizabeth": Mary, Kathy, Dawn, Jill, and Miss Rosemarie. It sure had been a long road to find these extraordinary people, who shared their gifts, but there they were. Thank you, God, for these people. Thank you for their presence in the life of Elizabeth.

It is funny how God's plans worked many times over the course of Elizabeth's life. John and I spoke about our desire to have more children, but we were scared. So scared to think about another child, who may in some way have needs similar to or greater than the ones Elizabeth faced. So as time went on, we gradually accepted the fact that, in the grand scheme of life, we were going to be a family of four; and we were thankful that we were happy together, and that we loved each other so much. Well, here comes the little twist to the story.

It started out with my "just not feeling well"; that feeling and four home pregnancy tests confirmed that I was, indeed, pregnant. Talk about surprised and happy! That was us. We truly were shocked. And, yes, if I shoved the test at John before for our first *two* children, I am sure I positioned this one a mere inch away from his eyes! When John gets nervous, he has a tendency to run his hands through his hair. Well, by the end of this evening, his hair looked like the hair of a mad scientist. And our moments of happy were then replaced by pragmatic thinking, like *Okay, I am going to be forty when I deliver, I am still on the antianxiety meds. Oh my God, I am pregnant...* And over and over, those thoughts went round and round in our heads.

The next morning, I quit my antianxiety meds cold turkey. (For the record, it is not recommended to do it this way and, yes, John is a doctor and told me to taper it down but I could not take it, knowing it was going into this new child.) I made an appointment with my doctor, and I began to pray. Yes, I prayed every day before, but now I was in a constant state of prayer. I knew this pregnancy was a gift from God, but I just prayed for a healthy child. That was it. I went to Mass every morning and prayed from my mother's manual of prayers. I wanted to be peaceful. But I was scared.

My beautiful mom came with me to every appointment I had with my doctor. I was too scared to go alone, and my mom always made me feel calmer just being there. Thank you again, Mom, for being there and for being that person for me. I love you more than I can say.

I asked Mary what she thought this child would do to Elizabeth, and she said, "This baby will help her grow, because now she will be the 'big' and she can help the baby and she will feel great to do it." I took some comfort in that, and I continued to go to church, ready the house for this new child, and keep our home humming along as best as I could. (I also ate every fruit and vegetable I could get my hands on!)

I remember telling my mom about this pregnancy and her look of surprise. She and I were at one of Emily's swim meets, and I asked her if she would like to be a Mimi again, as she is the best one in the world, and it took her a second. Then she got it! I also told her that night that John and I wanted the baby baptized right away. I wanted to give the baby right back to God. I said, "This baby is God's gift to us and I want to thank Him by holding up this child and giving God thanks."

Well, all that I wanted happened. Except this new little one must have decided that we seemed like so much fun that he needed to join us early, as in six weeks early. Yes, he was born weighing five pounds five ounces and at thirty-four weeks. So he had a week stay in the NICU. And yes, he was baptized there. He was given back to God in an incubator. We named him Michael. And he was healthy and well.

He was one of our three gifts from God, and he really was sent to all of us for a reason. John and I got so many laughs and giggles and fun from him. He brought a joy to this house that was so needed. And Emily got to have a sibling who, from the start, adored, loved, and hugged her. I was so thankful Emily got to have this, as she had certainly ridden out the storm that was her sister's life.

I love watching Emily with him. It makes my heart smile. I love watching John play with him. John looks like a kid again when he does, and I was so happy he got to be a father again, this time to a wonderful little boy. Michael loves his dad so much. I love watching my mom and dad love him up. They can't be away from him for too long, or they get withdrawal symptoms. They worked their Mimi and Popi magic on him too. He loves their house, and he absolutely loves them.

As for our Elizabeth, he has been magic. She loves him, and he calls her his best friend. She grew in ways I never knew she would because of him. She turned into the "big," and she loves the role. Not to say that some jealousy issues did not rear their ugly heads. Like when she decided to hug him around the neck just a little too hard. She said it was just because she loved him so much. We, however, knew otherwise. Thank you, God, for this Michael, his gifts, and for the family that had now become a family of five.

So what a year this has been; Elizabeth continued on to do so well in her year at school. She made so many gains. She read better and wrote better, and she acted so much more her age. We were proud and excited, to say the least. Her teachers told us she would be a second grader next year. But not before we had one heck of a ninth birthday party.

Knowing When to Let Go
and What to Hold on To

Happy birthday number nine to our school girl! One thing that is great about a summer birthday is the chance to have a great backyard party. I had had two small parties for her, but this year we decided to have a huge party to celebrate her successful first year in school. We invited some friends from school, some friends from the swim club, some of my friends and some of Emily's friends. This little child had two huge bouncers, water games, and a pyramid of cupcakes. She played all day and all evening on those bouncers. She had what I still feel is the best birthday time, ever. She was so tired the next day that she actually dragged her feet instead of walking, and she stayed in her pajamas all day. But it was worth it, let me tell you.

All this summer long, we swam, and Elizabeth took more swimming lessons, but due to some sensory issues, she was unable to put her head under the water. The instructor was very patient and understanding, but nothing we said or offered in the way of motivation (read: bribe) would make Elizabeth change her mind.

I still say to those in a similar position, these sensory issues do abate, but they are still part of your child; and with some new things, they will be brought back out. It is sometimes very hard to see her seem afraid, but it is who she is, and I have to be ready to try things to help her overcome whatever she is afraid of. Sometimes I can do it, and sometimes I cannot. She still shuts down when she is over-the-top scared, and that is when I usually know to get her out of a situation, and we'll talk about it later. Sometimes telling her what to expect or what we are going to do in a situation eases her discomfort. There is no real easy way or guarantee of a success. But at least we all know her signs, and she has great language to convey her feelings. Those are two things we did not have when she was a little girl.

I am telling you about this swimming situation only to be honest with the fact that Elizabeth was still Elizabeth. She still had, and always will have, her two disorders. And as she grew, the things she needed to learn and achieve were growing more complex, and those were things we had to help her get through and learn. It seemed daunting and overwhelming if I took in the whole picture, so I tried to see just a bit into the future and deal with it. I prayed for guidance and strength. As she got older, she was so much easier to reason with and to talk to, so we continued to build on that; and, so far, we were doing quite well.

I have quite happy memories of this summer. We had a healthy, little Michael, and lots of playtime together. Miss Rosemarie spent a great deal of time, both tutoring Elizabeth and swimming with her and Emily. This worked out great for me because I could relax and know my girls were having a fun time. I must say, seeing Michael grow really brought to light just how bad Elizabeth's disorders were. Michael was the calmest baby and so happy to be hugged. He was and is such an easy child to teach or simply spend time with. In my mind I see how Elizabeth was at the same age, and I cannot believe the difference between the two. I was ever so thankful that he was healthy and happy. I will say, this summer was great.

This year, as we entered another year of school, I decided to let Elizabeth take the bus. She was so excited, and I was so nervous that I asked Miss Rosemarie to follow the bus to the school to make sure she was tucked safely into the school the first two days. Miss Rosemarie did this, and we both laugh at how Elizabeth looked getting off the bus at school, with her huge backpack and her little legs.

I learned to become friendly with the bus drivers (I recommend this to all who need that extra, watchful eye on your child), and I made a point to call the drivers in early August to ask if Elizabeth could have the front seat. And I am so happy to say they all had been so kind and watchful of her. Some were even so kind as to give me their cell phone numbers to reach them, if I really needed to tell them something. And it turned out, she did great and loved riding the bus. Most kids don't like the bus; Emily had been known to show up on bended knees with her head bowed in the morning, asking for a ride to school, but not Elizabeth. She loved it. I was happy she did, and it was one more thing off my list of "Things to Worry About."

To this day, though, I still prefer having her to sit up front, and she loves to do this, as she tells the bus driver which children are absent that day so the driver does not make any unnecessary stops. And it keeps her from being in the middle of the bus, where she would be vulnerable to teasing or worse. (Sadly, this is a very big reality in our world now, so it pays to acknowledge it and be proactive.) So now we have her in her second grade room, and I made a very big error this year that I never made again.

I think that her first grade year was so full of firsts and new things that I, for the moment, just relished it all (and gave birth). I was so thankful for each day and each achievement that I did not really think about what the next year would bring, what goals to push for, or what I really expected of the school. I think I thought that they would handle it well and adjust the curriculum to challenge her at the next level, and that they would push her a bit to achieve more.

I learned that, like in the previously stated chapters, I needed to be those three steps ahead. Maybe because the first year was so good, I thought I could pass the baton to them a little bit, but I could not. I needed to think about the future; I needed to figure out what I wanted. I needed to really review the new IEP side by side to the old one, and see just what new goals there were. I needed to see if there was a sensory diet component in the IEP. I needed to educate the O.T., if needed, in the areas of her sensory needs. I needed to tell the speech person about all the oral motor exercises we did at home, and ask if they could follow up with them at school.

Basically, I needed to be what I was before, only now from my home, while trusting others. I would need to call often or communicate often, and it would just have to happen. I would just have to resign myself that I could not relax yet, not even a little bit. Sounds good, doesn't it, all that stuff that I should have done or been doing? Well, I got those things done, only not this year. No, this year I really made some errors.

I knew that Elizabeth's homeroom would change, but she would still have her same aide and the same special education teacher. Her aide, by the way, was a very nice and kind lady. She lives in our community and has children who go to our school system, and she was actually a friend of Denise's. I remember meeting her the first time and not fully getting that I would be entrusting my child to her. I thought, *How will it work?* and *Will she understand Elizabeth's ways?* I did not need to worry; she was a good fit for Elizabeth in the first year. I was actually so thankful to have her, and I made sure I often told her so. And I wrongly assumed the homeroom teacher would be talked to by the special education teacher and would know what to do to motivate Elizabeth or to encourage her during the times she was in her room.

But it did not happen. Elizabeth had her aide with her, so I knew she was being watched, but what I did not understand was why she was not being pushed to achieve even more goals. I would see her work come home, and it was the same as the year before. And when I asked her about her day, she would say she was in the special education room all day, instead of in those areas where she would be mainstreamed. I wanted her to be with typical kids and have experiences with and exposure to them. I wondered what I should do. Complain and make them feel defensive or angry, or trust their decisions?

I knew that if she was pushed too hard, she would shut down; and that would definitely be a problem. But I just got the feeling that she was allowed to do or not do things as she chose, and that was okay with everyone. And for those who didn't know, she was not one to seek out the new things. She would very comfortably settle into what she knew and could do well. So without someone to encourage her or figure out learning strategies for her, she would happily do all the things she knew without the stress of learning new things.

So that was why the work was the same. And she had no choice but to listen when the teacher told her which classroom to go to. That was why she ended up in the special education room instead of the mainstream rooms, as was promised.

I used to talk to her aide upon pick-ups last year, but now that she was taking the bus, I lost that opportunity.

I lost my day-to-day update. I actually waited until the conference time in November to meet face-to-face with the teachers. That was a full three months of school later. I remember the conference time and talking about how she was doing. I was told it had been a good year so far, and she seemed to like the kids at the school. Okay, that was good, but she was still doing the same things as last year and, when I mentioned this, I was told, "She is still mastering these skills." I guess I knew she needed extra time, but I struggled with her needing this much time. I really did not know how I felt upon leaving the conference.

I really had a hard time being upset since everyone was very nice, kind, and calm, but it seemed no one wanted to go that next step in getting Elizabeth to achieve. My thinking went along the lines of *She did well last year so now she is comfortable, let's raise the bar and encourage her, and let's go.* (Remember, I hate the thought of wasted time.) I will admit, it does take more thinking and definitely more work. I had been doing this her whole life, and I knew how very much work it was and, above all, you needed to believe in the ability of the person you were teaching and working with. And on many an occasion, it did cross my mind that maybe they really did not believe in her abilities to the degree that I did, and maybe they were teaching her with another mindset entirely.

I just didn't know. I knew that each year brought more advanced skills on the state standards, but with her IEP goals changing very little, I wondered what she was learning. What was hard here was, again, getting the teacher and special education teacher to agree to try different things, different learning strategies to help Elizabeth learn.

I did not push the issue this year (novice mistake); I did not go to the school to check in with the teachers (novice mistake). And I accepted what they did for Elizabeth as right (novice mistake, and one I never made again). Everything I learned over the years had only strengthened me in my ability to advocate for her and her needs. I think this was my first taste of feeling very much alone while in the presence of some fine educators. I have since learned to be much more watchful and much more of a presence in the school.

For those who feel the same way, I say go to the school and spend some time talking to the special education teacher and the mainstreamed teacher about your wishes and goals. I am not talking official IEP goals, just the ones you have for day-to-day interactions and occurrences. Use a conversation notebook to communicate daily. And do not be afraid to put your requests out there. It is your child. You really need to keep a watch on all parts of your child's day. And do not hesitate to discuss problems or concerns as they arise. I hate to say this, but this school year, in terms of academics especially, was mostly just wasted time. I will say that I learned as I went and, for sure, I learned this year.

This year, something sad and something happy happened. The sad part was that Miss Dawn was no longer doing private speech due to her taking a position with a local school. I really felt bad about this one because she was so nice and so kind. I knew I would miss her and all the good things she brought to Elizabeth. We wished her well, and then we were minus one of our friends and speech therapists combined. But I have learned from this journey that people are with us on our walk for however long they are supposed to be, and when something occurs to change their path and, thus, our path, I feel it was meant to happen at that time. I thank Dawn for all she gave to Elizabeth and to us.

The good thing that happened was that I had this idea to help Elizabeth, with her gross motor work related to gym activities. John and I are very big into working out, and we have a trainer whom we love. I asked him if he would consider working with Elizabeth to achieve some goals related to her big muscle groups. Maybe he could help her achieve goals like jumping rope or skipping, etc.—just the major things that one would run across in a typical gym class at the elementary level. He said he would, and I was excited.

Terry is the kind of man who is kind and caring, and he showed this all to Elizabeth as he worked with her. He made up a routine for her, and he broke down each skill into manageable bits, which they practiced and mastered before moving on to the next. Terry talked to Mary and got her help in planning what skill to attempt first, and Mary also gave him the background of Elizabeth's disorders. She told him how to deal with her anxiety. And after our appointment with Mary in October, she gave him some ideas of the exercises to add to his list. Our current assignment from Mary was really about gross motor work and a new oral motor protocol. So I was happy to have Terry hear the latest ideas from Mary.

Well, this move to have Terry help her has proven to be so wonderful. She enjoys her time with Terry and has mastered a number of new skills, and they continue to this day to work together and to make gains. I am so pleased to say that Terry enjoys working with her and seeing the gains she makes. He even thanked me for this chance to work with her, as it helped him grow as a trainer. It is kind of funny, but just as I sit back and think that I am content in what I am doing, an idea will pop into my head, and I will feel the need to investigate the thought. This is exactly how it went for me with Terry. I think for sure, I am always evaluating our current situation and thinking if it needs some adjusting or some tweaking. I say thank you to Terry for taking the time to help us and this little child. We so appreciate all his efforts.

For those in a position like we were and the need for some good basic skills are there, maybe it is worth considering someone like Terry. They have such a great background knowledge of the body and the muscles, and they can help with these skills. It has worked for us. And to this day, it is still working for us.

Sometimes, as I get the ideas to do something or call someone, and I really wasn't even thinking about it, I feel like God is guiding me. I pray often for just that. I always find that when I follow up on those things that have just come to me, they seem to always work out well.

So back to the school year. Well, it continued on in about the same manner as I previously described. And I was actually quite happy to see the school year end. I knew that the next year, I would be ready. I would not say it was a bad year, just a year that I wish had gone very much differently. And remember how I said we had our team of people? Well the line-up changed a little bit, didn't it, with the loss of Dawn and the addition of Terry? But Kathy, Jill, and our Rosemarie were still here. We were seeing Kathy for speech once a week and Miss Jill twice a month.

I think one of the most interesting parts of my time with Elizabeth now is seeing how strong she has become. I see her at school, dressing up for parties, doing the holiday parades, getting on stage for the Christmas play, and talking so much to her teachers and us. But because I am me, I still look at her and see certain things I want her to do better. I want her to look at people more when she talks; I want her to sit quietly when it is appropriate. I want her to lose some of her resistance to new things.

But what was amazing about my wish list now, as opposed to before, was that the things on it now were smaller in scale and more fine-tuned. She needed to learn the subtleties of behaviors and social activities, not how to use scissors. And in some way, isn't that what we all teach our children as they grow? I feel that due to her delays, both in talking and in achieving any motor skills, we were just at it a bit later than the rest of the typically developing world.

One of the problems with trying to guide and teach so late was that the behaviors she had were kind of habitual ones now and, therefore, harder to break or change. I found myself correcting and reminding her to "think and act properly." I needed a way to break some of those habits, and my current reward system was not enough. Now it needed more *oomph*. So Mary and I discussed changing her sticker chart to something more age-appropriate, yet motivating to her. We picked stringing beads.

I was using a list of desired activities to assess Elizabeth's behavior, but they were a more advanced list of activities and behaviors; and as we went down the list nightly we talked, and if she and I agreed she did this or that well, she got a bead to string and, with so many, (you can pick your number, we picked sixty-five), she picked out a reward coupon. She loved it! The stringing was good for her hands; the counting was good practice. We did it by fives and tens, and the talking was good back-and-forth turn-taking. Plus, it reinforced whatever things were the "current" things I wanted to have her do or not do. I even turned it into a motivator for proper behavior in public and home, as she would lose her beads if she chose to act improperly in public or toward her siblings. We talked about our expectations of her, and she was so smart, she understood so well.

To this day, we still do these beads and the chart of current behaviors has changed countless times, but it works. It is fun for me to have this time with her to talk and to motivate her, and it is so helpful in so many ways. I am so proud of her. She will always have her special ways, but she knows how much we believe in her and her abilities. I know as she grows, we will keep guiding her. But guess what? We are guiding Michael, and we are guiding Emily too! Don't all children have their own set of needs and their own time lines? Thank God, we really have come this far.

Too Much Moving and Shaking from Elizabeth and Too Little from the School

Happy, happy birthday to our ten-year-old. Wow! Double digits. This little child wanted a huge, outdoor blow-up waterslide for this year's present. Can you believe what that means? She wanted to climb up a wiggling, air-filled monstrosity, get to the top, get squirted on the way down a fast slide, all in her bathing suit and all by herself. So, of course, we said yes! She had always loved the bouncy places when we went there to play, so I thought she would *like* it, but she *loved* it; and it was great fun for us to see her play with Emily for hours. And Michael was happy just to be outside swinging and playing, so it really was a happy time for us.

"The best summer story" started off with my idea that camp would be fun for Elizabeth this summer. She could have something that was her very own, and she could go by herself, no aide. Well, she really wanted to go. So I got a copy of our local magazine for parents and read about summer camps. I found out that the place where Elizabeth went for the kindergarten program also had a summer camp. So one phone call later to her same teacher, and we had her enrolled and ready for a summer of fun.

We went that first day, and Elizabeth walked right into the play area with the kids and started to swing. That was it. I was beyond thrilled. Of course, I had to call mid-morning to check on her, and they said she was having a great day and doing all that the other kids were. I went to pick her up at 11:00, and found out she wanted to stay for lunch with the kids.

So as I went to talk to the director about this, she rushed over to me first, smiling ear to ear, and she said how much she could not believe her eyes that this child was the same one she saw in kindergarten. She said she could not believe all the changes she saw, and that it was like Elizabeth was a new child. I was so happy to hear these words because when you are in the forest, you do not see the trees, and I was *way* deep in the forest. So it felt extra great to hear this from a person who had not seen her in a long while. Yes, I think this qualifies as the best summer story yet.

Elizabeth continued to go to camp all summer for four days a week, and she had herself a big blast doing it (and no aide). I loved knowing she could do it all by herself.

Before I continue to talk about the next part of our story, I need to say I was so proud of her, and I so much wanted her to continue to make changes and gains; but there were still some things about her that I could not seem to affect change in, and one of them was her need to move, to fidget, and the positioning of her hands as she walked.

The other was her automatic "no" to me. I asked the camp director about the "no phenomenon," and she said they had very little trouble getting her to try things. Miss Rosemarie said the same. So I got it now—it was *me* she did this for.

This summer, I started to get the fact that she was better in some situations when I was *not* there. Yes, very weird to me too, especially from the child who was glued to me for the first two full years of her life. "Sounds kind of like a typical child to me," said Miss Rosemarie when I asked her about it. "Children do better for others than their parents many times."

I had to take a moment's pause on this one, and I filed the information away for future use. She even asked Miss Rosemarie, "Do you think Mommy will be proud of me?" I almost felt sad when she asked that, because she put so much weight into how I was feeling about her, and I was always proud of her. It was without a doubt that she and I definitely had our own dynamic together. I mean, we really had been through the fire together and had come out on the other side.

In reality, no one else I knew had this same relationship with their child as I did with our Elizabeth. It was weird right now, because she told me "no" a lot and acted difficult for me, but at the same time she wanted so much for me to be proud of her. I found myself getting mad at her and her attitude, and I struggled with how to deal with my anger and frustration.

I can honestly say that before this, I did not get really frustrated by her and her behaviors (I felt a lot of things, trust me, but frustrated was not one of them). I think because she was such a mystery to us and that we were so deep in our world, I was simply finding our way. I think fear and exhaustion were a more apt description of my feelings. I also knew she could not help how she felt or acted, so to get mad at that point would have been so wrong.

Having said that, I knew now she *could* control herself and she *could* tell me how she felt, but she was *choosing* to act a certain way with me and no one else, and I was not overreacting to her. Seriously, it really was *no one* else. This is where I need to thank John for being the happy place for Elizabeth, for taking her on those one-on-one walks and calming down her thoughts. Thank you for letting me vent to you my frustrations and fears.

I was told Elizabeth was delightful at school, with Kathy, Miss Rosemarie, and Miss Jill. I had such a hard time dealing with how she was acting to me. Why did she worry about making me proud, then proceed to be so negative and angry with me? On a certain level, I wondered if she was angry at me for pushing her so hard and for always raising the expectations.

On another level, I wondered if she was just tired of me and all my reminders on how to act, talk, behave. (I am actually tired of hearing myself, but I can't take off my own head, so I am stuck hearing it too.) I know this kind of sounds like a typical child. Maybe that is part of it too. But I could not help but think it was more. I never really expected her to turn on me this way. I guess I had hoped she would be happy that we did all we did for her and be happy we believed in her so much.

I was not sure how to handle this change in Elizabeth, and I wish I could say I did it with grace and ease, but I did not. Instead of being calm, I would engage in her comments and then either I would become angry, or she would have ended up saying something very wrong and then be sent to her room, writing for a punishment. I was very surprised at this turn of events, let me tell you. Why wasn't I getting to see the delightful Elizabeth? Why wasn't I getting to see her do her work easily and happily? Didn't I kind of deserve it after everything she and I had been through? I thought I would get to see the prize at the end. The one I worked for so long and hard, but right now she kept it hidden from me pretty well. She and I now seemed to have another thing to work on, and that was finding our way in this new relationship we had.

It took us a good while to find our way again. I decided to reward Elizabeth for good responses, try to ignore the minimal infractions, and only address the big ones. I also tried to help her identify her feelings, both verbally and with a picture chart of feelings, so that she and I could talk about them. And lastly, I decided when I was mad

I was going to hug her. Yep, instead of separating, I was going to hug her and kiss her and tell her I loved her. I found that when I was mad or hurt, this could be one of the hardest things to do. Separating felt so much better, but I forced myself to hug her and kiss her and tell her I loved her, and I will say it had worked the best of all the things listed above. It seemed to take the edge off of her attitude instantly. And we are still working on this classically challenging relationship that is number one, mother and daughter, and number two, me and Elizabeth.

If you ask Elizabeth one of our prayers she says every night, she will tell you we pray for God to "help Mommy and me find our way together to be best friends forever." And we pray this every night. And I am sure we will always be working on "us." It is so important to both of us, and I am sure that prayer will be used a great deal.

When I speak of certain relationships, I think of Emily, and how she is growing, and our relationship. I know we have no way of doing this, but I bet if we could go back in time, and Elizabeth was born as a typical child, I am sure my relationship with Emily would be so different from the one it is now. Emily and I talk so much and about so many things, which is a gift, to say the least. But because we always have to be so aware of her feelings due to her sister and her needs, we have allowed Emily an openness for discussion that is unique and one that I am proud of.

It initially started out that with us talking about Elizabeth and all of Emily's feelings, her real feelings, no holds barred. Then it grew from there, and now we really have no topics that are off-limits. I love spending time talking with Emily, and I love hearing what is going on in her life, and I love the freedom we give her to talk about her thoughts and opinions. I can see this as part of the good that has come from Elizabeth.

I did not forget to address the two issues mentioned before, one being the fidgeting and moving and the other being the positioning of her hands as she walked. I tell you about these things at this point because, after the best camp story, you might feel that she is now "all better." It would be unfair of me to present things that way. If you were to see her, you would initially see a beautiful, blue-eyed, brown-haired child. Then you might notice her hands were up. Or that she was moving a lot. She would show you some of her disorders when you engaged her in conversation. Or if you asked her to do something, she may look afraid.

She still had her disorders, as I have said before, and they did show their faces at certain points and times, just to a much lesser degree. I think so many good things happened to her, and so many great changes occurred in her, one after the other, that it felt great to be excited about where we were, to look back and be thankful we weren't still there, and then in a month feel that same way again. And so on and so on.

But now it seemed the gains were harder to achieve than the ones we made earlier on. I suppose it was because the areas I wanted to correct were those that seemed to be ingrained. I am simply being honest. After all, she was soon to begin third grade, and she needed to be aware of these issues.

Elizabeth's hands were in what Mary called the "high guard," or basically arms up and hands about shoulder level. Mary said this was related to Elizabeth's sensory issues, kind of to protect herself from something new, and was now a habit. She could control this when she was thinking about it, but if she got distracted, then she would do it again, and I wanted this to go away. She also still moved and fidgeted a lot. I didn't know the reason for these things, but they just flat out made me nuts. I really wanted to find a way to extinguish these above stated behaviors, but how? The beads helped with the little day-to-day things we wanted to reinforce, but we needed something more to help with these big things.

I talked to Mary about the hands, and she and I discussed my using a hand signal for Elizabeth, one that would let her know she needed to control her arms and hands but would allow me to do it without words, so it would be less noticeable that I was correcting her. I talked to Elizabeth about this signal, and she said she understood. We picked a signal that she could see and understand, and we were off.

So now, in addition to my verbal reminders before we went somewhere, and the behavior notebook, when it was needed, we used these signals. I had a few, actually. The first went very well, so I added more. For instance, the signal for her hands was that I simply looked at her and pointed down. The other one I used a great deal was tapping the back of my wrist. This meant "think and act properly." She knew what these meant, and she did it. It was a nice reminder and *quiet*. On good days, I used one signal once in a while; and on bad days, I felt like the first base coach on a baseball team, with all the signals I was throwing out. But they did work. I liked them because no one else knew what I was saying to her.

So for those who think this may be an idea for you and your child, try one. See how it goes. You may be surprised how nicely this works. I like having the beads to reinforce what I do and what I expect from her each day. I even have the signals replacing the notecards we were using. We are still using the signals, and the targeted behaviors have gone so far down, and she is very, very aware of how she presents herself, which is a good thing. She, herself, wants to act well and properly, and that in and of itself is a huge gift. I can really work with her when the desire comes from her and not just me.

If you remember, some time ago I talked about Mary and I discussing diets and supplements for Elizabeth. I was not really ready at that point, and now when I told Mary about these fidgets and movements, she mentioned that maybe I should think about getting Elizabeth an appointment with a biomedical doctor who could look at her diet and see if anything we were or were not doing could be adding to this fidgeting and movement issue. I talked with John, and we agreed to make an appointment with this doctor who ended up being an hour away. We wanted the first appointment of the day, so we had to wait until March of the following year to get a date. I will revisit this topic later, but at least we addressed our biggest concerns.

Wow, from the best summer camp story to all this other stuff! But it is what occurred and it all needs to be said, as it all happened. So I left off with the summer being great, and it was. The kids all had fun together, and I had noticed that Elizabeth was addicted to her little brother. She loved him so much and where he was, she was. I got a big charge out of how she talked to him and the funny things she said. She really had quite a cute sense of humor. Emily was thrilled to have these siblings, and she just thrived on the role of big sister, let me tell you. So we were thankful and happy for sure.

So now we were entering fall. We find out that Elizabeth had one of the kindest, gentlest third grade teachers available, and for that I was thankful. I went into the school year with a new focus. I wanted to be more involved and more aware of the day-to-day activities. I began a conversation notebook where I could write my concerns or questions and get a response from Elizabeth's aide each day. I asked for the special education teacher to again reinforce that Elizabeth had her hands down, and that she would be "pushed" a bit more in her work. I had made these same requests last year. I felt that the follow-up at school could make or break a behavior.

Actually, I felt pretty good going into this year, until I started to see how nervous or stressed Elizabeth was when she came home. She was so stressed she would march in, toss and or slam her backpack, and answer any question or hello in a horrible way. I thought, *Okay, we will let this go one or two days.* But then she cried during her homework time, and she was bristly, as I liked to say, all evening. And those lovely nos were flying all over the house. Yuck! I tried not to react, oh did I try, but then it got to be too much, and I would yell or take away a privilege for being rude. And yes, I tried to hug this one off too, but it went deeper than a hug could affect. I offered her the chance to brush herself and sometimes she would, sometimes she would not. I was in a true quandary at this point. I hated to have the house be in a state of upheaval, and it certainly felt that way.

I had a renewal date for the IEP in September, which meant that we had to sign a new one each September. I talked to Mary about these behaviors, and she said we should get a brushing protocol set up for Elizabeth in her school day, along with sensory diet changes that should calm her. So on the date of the IEP signing, I was there alone (I told John not to take the day off). After all, I would only be making some small changes to the IEP on the education goals and adding the brushing, etc.

Well, that decision was wrong. Very wrong. I entered the room and sat down, surrounded by the entire IEP team. And when I made my request for the brushing and sensory diet, I received a response from some members of the IEP team I never would have imagined. My recollection of the conversation is like this: "I see you want the school to do extra work for you child so that you could have her come home and be calm for you. I don't think that is the way it works, Mrs. Gianetti."

I had one member of the team actually ask me about Mary's qualifications. Needless to say, I was so very taken aback. I went away angry, hurt, and with a sense of disbelief.

I could not believe that they thought I wanted them to fix her. I asked for her to be brushed three times during the day for a grand total of three minutes of time. And I asked for a sensory diet. And, let's see, I do what for her at home! I phoned the school the next day and spoke to one of the members who had made the affronting statement. I told that person I did not appreciate the comments made nor the attitude they had for me in front of the other IEP team members. I also invited them over to our house so they could see all we do for our child and be part of our evening, and then they could decide if indeed we were wanting the school to do all the work.

I did receive an apology during the phone call. I asked the person to tell the other members of the IEP team that we had talked so that they could know I called and addressed the poor attitude given to me. *We are on the same team*, I thought, *so why the resistance?* And I guess this was where I learned to be ready to fight for my wants and wishes for my child. Oh, and by the way, those particular team members have not yet taken me up on that offer to come over.

I did not sign the IEP that day, for sure, and I did bring John the next time we went, and I had Mary on speakerphone. I also had Kathy there, and I believe I had a parent advocate also, and together we got the brushing protocol set up, along with a delightful sensory diet and oral motor activities; and we agreed I would send a check-off form for each of the above that would be sent home daily to let me know when Elizabeth brushed herself or when they did the other things. It took a great effort and John asking one of the IEP team members not to roll her eyes at the comments Mary made about the brushing protocol. John simply, and with the directness of a fine physician, asked, "It's simple, are you or are you not going to brush her? Just answer the question." It took the whole room by surprise, and it felt absolutely great to have us leading this conversation now.

We were able to get what we wanted, but the sad part was why did we, and do we, have to fight so hard for things that help the child? Weren't we all supposed to be on the same team, and wasn't the whole goal here to help the child? I don't know, but as I said, I learned to be ready. Sadly, I had to be ready to fight and push and demand at any given moment.

If there's one thing I have learned from these IEP experiences, it is that the parents have the power, for lack of a better word. We have the ability to call a meeting when needed, to ask for changes to the IEP to suit our child's needs at a given moment, and the power to sign or not sign the IEP. Ultimately yes, it needs to be signed, but until it suits your child's needs and is satisfactory to you and your significant other, then you have the power to say, "I am not signing it until ... it is done." I would never have thought of taking such a hard stance or having such a hard edge to my advice, but it is seriously how I am now. And I made mistakes that I hope others can avoid.

I also advise anyone scheduling an IEP meeting to take your significant other with you, along with any other therapist or tutor. You can use their expertise to help you make your case for your child, and you will definitely be thankful for their support. And lastly, Mary's credentials were given to the that team member, and I myself found them to be very impressive. This same team member has proven to be a wonderful member of Elizabeth's team.

I thought this was a very interesting start to the school year, but surprisingly things started to smooth out. Elizabeth came home calmer, and I was able to implement the recordkeeping for the oral and sensory protocols. Elizabeth was enjoying her days at school and even got voted class leader by her classmates in her homeroom later in the year, which I was told does not happen to everyone. So we were proud and excited for her. She was still spending too much time in the special education room and not with the traditional children, but this seemed to be one area I really could not change, other than to ask about it often; I really could not control whether or not the teacher or the aide decided to bring them back to the special education room.

Secretly, I wondered if it was not just easier overall to have them in the special education room, where no one had to make sure they were doing what the other kids were doing, or making sure they were not being disruptive. I say "disruptive" here not for Elizabeth, who definitely needed reminders to sit still but who was and is a young lady, but for the other three kids who traveled with the same aide.

But again, I really could not affect much change in this one area. I do know my heart would sink when I asked Elizabeth, for instance, where she was for indoor recess, only to find out she was in the special education room instead of with the traditional kids. I remember asking if she could be mainstreamed in a class like science or social studies. Not so much to learn the content, but just so she could see how to act and behave in a traditional class. But I was told they thought the pressure of the classroom would be too much for her. I disagreed, but did not push the issue. I thought that with adaptations, she could learn key concepts and ideas. I did not win this battle, though.

For those who are in a similar position, it is good to know what I did not know at the time. But the special education teacher, sometimes now called the intervention specialist, is the one responsible for the adaptations and for being the liaison between the teacher in the traditional classroom and the special education child. And this takes work. A great deal of work. And follow-ups and conferences with the teacher. So please know that the special education teacher really needs to be the kind who is ready and willing to do these things for your child. You may have to address this issue if he or she has not.

I wanted then, and still do now, for Elizabeth to shoot for the stars. I feel that any place new we go or anything new she tries, she will learn something. And that is a good thing.

So I wanted her in one of these classes to learn as much as she was able to. I sometimes wondered what was more of a reason for her not being in the room, the fact that she *really* could not handle it or the work that needed to done just for her to get her into that room.

As I am writing this story of my child, I go back and reread what I have already written. I think, *Wow, it really has been a big, long fight for her.* I believe in her, and I want her to have every chance there is to succeed. I promised myself we would be revisiting the issue of more main-streamed classes at a later time.

The winter was now upon us, and all was continuing. She was being tutored by Miss Rosemarie two times a week, and she was reading and writing better. She was going to Miss Jill once every two weeks now, and she was doing very well. She was very calm coming home and, according to my daily records, she was brushing herself every two hours and was doing her exercises to calm herself (like wall push-ups). The speech teacher was attempting to accomplish an oral motor protocol, but it was hard because this was one area that Elizabeth hated to work on.

I was happy with the events of the year, and I even wrote in my journal over the Christmas break:

> All I can say is that she was phenomenal! All break, she acted so big, so ten and so happy and appropriate. From the day she got off through Christmas Eve and Christmas Day. Loved her presents, loved putting cookies out for Santa and her note. She was so happy and fun. God bless her.

I love that journal entry. It makes me so happy and gives me a mental picture of our holiday time and how much she enjoyed it all. She was enjoying life fully now, she wanted to act well, she could do it now. She was happy. I remember many Christmases before when she would not touch an ornament or hang a candy cane. She said no to opening any gifts, or she would cry and we had to try very hard to pretend all was well for Emily's sake; Emily would be running around with a Santa hat on and hanging candy canes and singing, while Elizabeth would be behind a chair, and no amount of asking would get her to relax and enjoy it. But the door to that Elizabeth had closed, never to be reopened again.

I wrote before that we were waiting until March to have our meeting with the doctor who specialized in biomedical treatment of children with spectrum disorders. His office was about one good hour away. I talked to Mary about this appointment, as I was a breath away from canceling it. I did not want to go at all. All I could think about was the fact that I would not be willing to change Elizabeth's diet if that was his idea. Mary told me to go because he was about more than diet and he could assess Elizabeth and discuss supplements or things to add to her diet to help her system. And maybe help her body calm down. Remember all that fidgeting and moving? So we decided to go.

I remember one time trying to change Elizabeth's diet by taking out milk and wheat, which are considered two highly allergic substances. I wondered if they could be making her feel jumpy. I have never in my life been so crazy and, trust me, I have been knocking on the door of crazy plenty of times. But I could not find foods she would eat. I remember giving her rice bread, and the fact that she just looked at it on her dish. I got her favorite vegetable soup, only without the wheat, and she again just stared at it. So it became clear that I either had to abandon the new regimen or watch her watch her food all day. So I changed it back. Her hunger strike would have impressed Ghandi himself.

So this was why I very, very, very much did not want to try this again, if this was all that was going to be offered. And then how exactly would I change all the food in the house for all of us (which would have had to be done)? Remember, I had a toddler, who was munching on Cheerios half his day.

Oh, and another quick point of reference is that Elizabeth is hungry two-thirds of her life and eats like a teenage boy. Not many people can believe the amount of food she is able to eat and still stay on the thin side of normal. (She gets this metabolism from my mom. I think this is God's gift to her, as kind of a treat, given all the challenges she has had, but hey, that is just my theory.)

Biomedical treatment of children begins with a detailed evaluation of the child. I had to fill out a huge form, remembering details from my pregnancy with Elizabeth through the delivery, and then all sorts of details about her infancy, etc. It was a very complete history of Elizabeth's life. The doctor then recommended the testing he wanted done to see what was actually happening in the child's body. Based on these, the doctor then recommended as treatment nutritional supplements or vitamin supplements or detoxification of metals. This was a very simple definition of biomedical treatment. I used information given to us by our doctor but, please note, when we looked it up on the Internet, we saw many sites available for more information.

I guess now is a good time to say that the whole issue of biomedical treatment is one that is very controversial for sure. Some swear by it, and others condemn the doctors for preying on the hopes of desperate parents. I will at this time just tell our story. Everyone has their own thoughts and like I have said so many times, if something works or worked for you, then I feel it was meant to be, so enjoy the success that was yours.

Our story is that we went there with one thing in mind, and that was trying to find out why she fidgeted and moved so much. I did not want much more than that. I wanted her to feel calm inside, and thus present an outward calm. I was not wanting much more. The appointment went well over two hours, with much of it being talking between us and the doctor. And with John being a doctor, they could really get into the wheres, whys, and whats of the blood and body. We left there with two boxes of test kits and a slew of prescriptions for blood and urine tests, even one for stool.

I was hungry (and not for rice bread, let me tell you) and very overwhelmed. We went home, and I put all the boxes and papers in a pile to revisit in a day or two. I did get back to them, and we did do all the testing. It was very hard to get it all accomplished, but we did. The results came back, and it showed she had yeast showing up on all the tests that tested for it. Off the charts, it was shown. The doctor said a child who tested this positive for yeast was generally more irritated, antsy, and hard to settle. *Okay,* I thought, *I will buy that.* I even checked it out with my big brother, C.J., who is a brilliant pathologist, and he concurred.

So now what? Well, she got put on a slew of supplements, all designed to rid her body of the yeast. I decided to wait for summer to start implementing these and to do them one at a time to assess their effects on her. I kept very detailed records and notes. It was good I waited because, *yuck,* it was bad for her (nausea and flu-like for a few days). Then she was feeling okay, and we continued on the treatments.

It was also determined that based on her blood work, she had a need for some amino acids. I was told these would help her system achieve a state of calm. So we began those, also. And we had two creams to use two times a day. All in all, we ended up with twelve supplements. I did see her appear calmer, sitting better in church, etc., and I asked the school if she seemed different to them (I did not tell anyone we were trying this avenue), and they said, "Oh, yes, she just seems more peaceful." I asked Elizabeth how she was feeling, and she told me she did not feel nervous anymore. Okay, I will take it and be happy.

We stayed on the regimen for over one year and six months. And it was good in many ways, and wonderful to see her benefiting from the treatments, but hard in other ways, keeping up the schedule every day. I will say that Elizabeth was one heck of a good trooper about it all. I mean, would you want your mom to wake you up each day at five thirty with a small cup full of supplements that she would make you drink before your head really got off the pillow? Then I would rub cream on her back. And that was just one of five dosing times each day. I kept the schedule even if we went out to dinner or on vacation. I packed it all up and made sure she was on her supplements. I felt sure about what we were doing, so I gave it my all. I recorded any gains and any problems.

Besides the schedule as a downfall, I will also say that a big consideration would be the financial aspect. These supplements were in no way inexpensive, and they were all out of pocket costs, as were the appointments with the doctor, be they in his office or by phone call. I found out that every time I called the doctor, I was charged per fifteen-minute increments; so the one time we had a problem, I ran up a ninety-dollar bill. When it was time for a long appointment by phone, we were charged upwards of three hundred dollars. It really was expensive. I was surprised that any questions had a fee attached, since my husband generally answered questions when patients called free of charge. But I did not let it deter me, as I was seeing and hearing the results I wanted. I did mind the charges, but at the same time I was not letting that be a reason for us to stop.

I am being honest here, and the truth is that for anyone considering this avenue, and I know that so many are, cost is a factor. I fully get that so many people have gone into some serious debt for their child with special needs. I again am just giving my impression here and my story.

As summer approached, I would say that the third grade year ended well for Elizabeth. No major problems. She had her multi-factored evaluation in late winter of the year, which means she was tested again in the same fashion as she was in order to get into school three years ago. I found out that when the testing was done, it was good for three years. So I every three years, she would need to be retested. John and I decided that we were going to have her tested by someone other than those from the school system.

We thought it might be a better idea to have fresh eyes doing the test, and it would be nice to control the timing of the test and the day of the test. I had been told by the school that they were going to take her out of class every now and then to accomplish some of the testing. I thought that it might be harder on her to have to go between class mode and test mode until the testing was done; therefore, we arranged to have the testing done by a very nice lady affiliated with one of our special needs schools.

She tested Elizabeth in her office for the academic portion of the test and came to the same conclusion as the previous testing, which was not what wanted to hear. What I wanted to hear was, "Wow, this child has scores that are so much better than before!" So I was feeling bad about it, until she called me into her office to talk it over with me and she said something like, "Oh, Michele, if I could have only given her a hint or two, she would have done so much better. She really has the ability, and it is a shame I have to leave her score the way it is, but it is there."

I felt so much better after that. I asked if she could attend the meeting again with the whole IEP team (we all should have been close friends by now). We were going to have to discuss the testing, and she said she would and she did, and she told them the same thing she told me. So if it counted for anything, they all heard again of her ability, even if the score had to remain the same.

But I knew I was right. She had it in her, in there, and we were getting it out of her each day and with each effort we made. She was going to succeed.

I had a hard time at the end of this year because as fast as I think the year went, it needs to be said that Elizabeth's entire time at this elementary school had gone even faster. Next year, she would be in fourth grade, and that meant she would be done with elementary school. How was that for some time passing?

I was so proud of her. Elizabeth was one of the most well-known children in the school. When I would go in, I would see *everyone* saying hi to her, kids and faculty alike. She had a winning personality and was well-liked by everyone. I remember one particular teacher who had a reputation for being especially stern. This woman actually broke ranks when in our town's Fourth of July parade for the sole purpose of hugging a special little girl, who was Elizabeth. She was doing what was asked and doing well.

I find it hard to explain how I felt. But as good as she was doing, something was missing. I wished everyone would please do as we asked and would believe in her as deeply as we did. I think when those two pieces of the puzzle were missing, it was very hard to relax and fully enjoy the successes, as one can't help but wonder, *If those two pieces were here, where would we be then?*

I wanted so much for her to be mainstreamed in a science class, but I was told they thought it would not work for her. This year I asked for social studies, and I was again told no. Now I really could have pushed, and should have pushed, but this was where their belief in her should have kicked in and said, "Let's make it work for her. She deserves a chance to get whatever she can from any experience," and that did not happen.

Why not? Where was the belief? I had seen how hard we had to fight for her, and I saw how much monitoring it took on my end to make sure all was in order, that when I thought of the future, it made me take pause.

Having just said all that, I will say this year had taught us a lot. We were different now than at the beginning of the year. I was glad it all happened this early in the game, and that we learned how to be strong, so very strong for her. And we learned how to stay determined. Yes, it had been a year of learning, for sure.

Happy Birthday Number Eleven: Looking Forward to the Future— Middle School, Here we Come

I guess somewhere in the mixing, measuring, and demanding Elizabeth drink supplements, we wished Elizabeth a happy eleventh birthday. No seriously, we did have a great birthday. She had brunch with us and Mimi and Popi. Then we went berry picking with Uncle C.J. and Aunt Lyn. She had what she said was "the best birthday ever."

Just prior to that was a family vacation to Ocean City, and she loved it. It was our first vacation since having our little Michael, so we picked a beach within a day's drive. So Ocean City, it was. As was expected, Elizabeth would not get out of the water all week! For a point of reference, Michael would not get in the water because it was too choppy. He would not touch wet sand because he knew he was getting close to the water. Of course, he was only two. But there she was, out there and happy as a clam.

We even have a great restaurant story from this trip that tells a lot about Elizabeth. We were going into a very fancy seafood buffet. Michael had his own food to eat. Elizabeth fell in the "twelve and under" range. And then there was the issue of Emily, who was actually thirteen, but we decided to say she was twelve for two reasons. One, she was a very picky eater and would only eat a limited type of food, and two, she was a *very* picky eater.

We had never done this before and, after this story, we never will again. Emily also looked older than she was, so it was a bit of a push. Still, we tried it. The hostess asked us the children's ages, and we fibbed. We sat down, and all was going well until the waitress asked us the children's ages. When we told her, Elizabeth said, "So what, Emily is twelve years old now?" I was so close to laughing and so embarrassed that I did not say anything, and Elizabeth was kind enough to repeat the question. Well, I guess we said something, and the waitress left to get our drinks. But it was hilarious and embarrassing and yet so reaffirming of what was inside this child and what she took in just by being somewhere.

Elizabeth also got the award for the best car traveler, as Emily was coming down with a cold and was, how shall we say, very much the maligning child for close to six hours. So the gold star of the trip was proudly on Elizabeth's chart.

Our family is extremely close, and we have so much fun together, and it was true on this trip as well. We loved having this little Michael on his first trip to the beach. He hated the ocean, but it was so fun to see the kids together having fun and making memories with each other. I felt so thankful, so deep down inside, each time I heard them laugh or saw them hug each other because, truth be told, Emily could very easily have grown to resent her sister, and Elizabeth could have been an angry child. But it did not happen that way; they all three loved each other.

We arrived home from this trip to a full summer off together. Elizabeth was attending a different camp, still a traditional camp. She ended up having a great summer camp experience, and she loved it. She went four days a week. She had speech class with Kathy, and tutoring with Miss Rosemarie. As for the update on the sensory issues, we had a trip to Mary scheduled for late June.

It was on this trip that Mary and I discussed adding more thinking language to help instruct Elizabeth; so instead of saying, "Please behave in church," I was to ask, "How do you think you should act in church?" or "Let's think about some of the things you did that were proper."

Mary gave me a whole list of these thinking questions, and she gave me an updated oral motor protocol. Speech clarity had consistently been a challenge for Elizabeth, so we were always working on ways to help her become more clear and understandable. Mary also proactively gave me the name of a book called *Taking Care of Myself* by Mary Wrobel.

For those of you who need to talk to your child about self-care as they grow up, this is a great book and very easy to follow, as it is in easy-to-read sentences and easy to find areas of concerns. I think it is a good idea to start to introduce things way ahead of the time you think you may need them. This way the groundwork is laid several times before the actual time you need it, and then the anxiety will be lessened. Like I said before, we were still using the TLP™ program, as we are to this day.

I found myself amazed that this was all there was from Mary. I had one sheet of paper to do and think about. Times and care for this child were changing. They were requiring more thought, for sure, but they were so different than the first batches of information. This summer was a fun one full of mixed supplements, but still great.

As we entered the fall, I had another one of my ideas, and it goes a little something like this. I thought one of the biggest problems with last year was my inability to really follow Elizabeth's progress and just waiting until conference times. I knew the notebooks worked well, and I planned on using them for sure, but I needed more. I thought it would be a good idea if I could meet face-to-face with the special education teacher every three weeks. That way I could see the teacher three times in a grading period, and that way not much could really happen that I wasn't aware of; or if something was wrong, I could fix it or work on it. The same went for her schoolwork and her progress on her IEP goals.

So I did just that. I went every three weeks, and I felt so good being a bigger part of her school world. I found this to be very helpful, and I have continued this practice to this day. For those who need to feel more aware, I would so much recommend scheduling this time to meet with the special education teacher.

I loved hearing from the current teacher how Elizabeth was looking very calm, even more so than before. So I continued to believe in the supplements. I know our pediatrician was skeptical at best when we told her of our foray into the area of supplements, but I continued to believe in them. I was not sure how long we would continue them, as I could see clearly how hard it would be to keep up the schedule and the documentations, but for now I was pleased with the results.

As I reread my journal for her, I keep seeing small entries for each month, saying how calm she was and how well she was doing at school. I see the one for Christmas, and it says she was so happy all vacation and so appropriate. I had little else to say because I know I was so focused on recording the information I was seeking. I read over and over that she was happy, and I know we have done well by her.

As I get to the marker of spring, I see a note from her aide telling me just how much social growth she had seen in Elizabeth this year, and how proud she was of her. I know this year had been a good one in many ways.

But Elizabeth was not asked to be part of the fourth grade science fair. We were not given the option. I mean, maybe the thought of prepping something with a two-year-old as my apprentice may not have been my dream scenario, but I wanted her to have the chance. She needed to be part of all activities as much as possible. She needed the chance to live. I couldn't believe that even with my meeting every three weeks, I still missed out on this one. See how my guard cannot be let down?

I have mixed feelings about the end of this year. We are leaving the only school we have known, and I am now just really finding my "school legs," as it were, to know how to watch, handle, and manage all the things needed for this child, including all fairs and festivals. She will start middle school next year with a new school, new start time, new aides and teachers and yes, *science*, as well as home economics and art; she is going to be mainstreamed in there. It is a time for new everythings. I am sure we will have to find our way, but I also know she is getting all the chances she deserves. I want her to have a great summer and be ready to greet the next part of her life. Middle school, here we come.

Before I can go any further, I feel so strongly that I want to thank my mom and dad for their never-ending love and support of me and our family, and this little child my dad lovingly calls his "penny from heaven," because without them, I do not know how I would have made it. Thank you for all your hugs, advice, tissues for my tears, phone calls, and love. Thank you for being the very best Mimi and Popi any three children could ever have. You are loved, my dear mom and dad, so very much. And thank you to my two brothers and our Aunt Lyn for all you give and gave to us. For your love and for loving these kids who love you right back. God has sure provided us with a support system that rivals them all.

When I started out on this writing adventure, I was not quite sure what to pick as my ending point to this story about the first part of Elizabeth's life. I thought about it a great deal, and I decided to make the end point be the end of the fourth grade school year. *What a perfect point,* I reasoned, *as the teen years are ahead of us, and the elementary years are just now behind us.* So that is what I did. I say an "end point" to our story, but it really is not an end point because as I have continued to write, this beautiful little girl has continued to grow and change and soar. There are more stories after the fourth grade year to tell.

I look at the beginning words of this book and envision the little child placed on my stomach. And I look at the final few words of this book, and I struggle to believe that her life is in these pages. All of what she is, who she is, and what she has been through are here. Holding this book, I hold her life in my hands, a life that has been so much work, and such an exercise in catching up.

Prior to having children, I worked at an elementary school as a school nurse and I became dear friends with the speech teacher, Marilyn R. We stayed friends even after I had left to stay at home, after Emily's birth. She passed on some wonderful advice to me, way back when. And by way back when, I mean when I was not sure if Elizabeth had sensory issues or what her real problems were. She said, "Michele, whatever you do, enjoy her, love her. Time will pass, and you will know you did this."

I have often revisited that advice, especially when times were hard. And now, just like Marilyn said, time did pass, and you know what? I did do what Marilyn advised. I loved her. Things were not easy, but I saw the good in them and I thanked God for the good, and I enjoyed the good, and I loved her. Yes, I did. I know we did right by her. I see those bright eyes shining, and I hear her easy laugh and love her little hugs, and I know we did right by her. I see her having a future. I see her happy. Please always know, my precious Elizabeth, I believe in you.

Epilogue

Through the course of this book, I know I have given a number of therapies and ideas that we have tried, some with great success and others with a distinct failure. The ironic part of all this is that I am still learning as my child grows. I am still learning how to adjust and change our rewards and patterns as her needs dictate. Just yesterday, I spent forty-five minutes on the phone with Mary, talking about some things I have noticed in Elizabeth, and I came away both clear-headed and with four new adjustments to our current regimen.

I guess my whole point here is that I am still finding my way, and I am still looking for the next right move. We are in what I would compare to a chess game, with every move needing to be thought out and analyzed completely before it is made. As each move is critical for Elizabeth, I don't take my hand off the chess piece until I am sure I have weighed each outcome. It is long and hard, and no one is guiding me or saying, "Hey, here is what we did, try this." We are still on the journey, still making a new path.

I guess my final point in this last story is that I want to help those who may be back at our initial starting point, with no real path yet to be on. I want to tell what we tried. Maybe something will spark a thought for those who need help. I am by no means an authority or a therapist. I am a mom who wanted more for her daughter and who never wanted to settle. Once again, thank you for reading our story and taking the journey with us.

listen|imagine|view|experience

AUDIO BOOK DOWNLOAD INCLUDED WITH THIS BOOK!

In your hands you hold a complete digital entertainment package. In addition to the paper version, you receive a free download of the audio version of this book. Simply use the code listed below when visiting our website. Once downloaded to your computer, you can listen to the book through your computer's speakers, burn it to an audio CD or save the file to your portable music device (such as Apple's popular iPod) and listen on the go!

How to get your free audio book digital download:

1. Visit www.tatepublishing.com and click on the e|LIVE logo on the home page.
2. Enter the following coupon code:
   668c-d362-513f-60f1-8644-2183-930c-603b
3. Download the audio book from your e|LIVE digital locker and begin enjoying your new digital entertainment package today!